AF406881

Simply Teacher

The Life of Avis Carrington

Simply Teacher. The Life of Avis Carrington
Copyright©2021 by Hazel Lindo-Carrington

57 Newton Terrace
Christ Church
Barbados
BB17073

All rights reserved. The use of any part of this publication, reproduced, transmitted in any form or by any means, electronic, mechanical, photocopying, recording, or stored in a retrieval system, except for the purpose of review, without the prior written consent of the publisher or author, is an infringement of the copyright law.

ISBN# 978-976-96542-0-4

The incidental citation by contributors of works by other writers is intended to be for review or illustrative purposes only. The copyrights of the authors of said works are fully recognised.

This book is designed and typeset in Minion Variable Concept and Helvetica Neue by ArtsEtc Inc. Printed and bound in Barbados by COT Holdings Inc.

hlindocarrington@yahoo.com

Cover photo by Ronnie Carrington

Simply Teacher

The Life of Avis Carrington

HAZEL LINDO-CARRINGTON

Christ Church
Barbados

"Now, what really makes a teacher is love for the human child; for it is love that transforms the social duty of the educator into the higher consciousness of a mission." —Maria Montessori

Simply Teacher: The Life of Avis Carrington

Contents

*To my ninety-four-year-old mother, Reverend Desdemona
Lindo-Layne, who was denied a secondary education because of
her socio-economic status. After several years of serving in various
capacities at the Church of the Nazarene, she graduated in 1982
from Barbados Bible Training College (now Bethel Bible College of
the Caribbean, Barbados) with a Diploma in Theology.
It is on her shoulders that I stand.*

*To all teachers everywhere. The most important teaching resource
is the love you give freely from the heart.*

The Honourable Mia Amor Mottley,
Prime Minister of Barbados.

Foreword

I was not yet four years old when I first met Teacher, as she was known to her young students at Mrs Carrington's school. At that tender age, I could not have known she would have an indelible effect on my life. I am told that I refused to go to my class and followed her around for an entire week. I did settle down eventually, and my seven years' experience there left me with such a lasting impression, especially when I remained in the Common Entrance class for two years, being too young to take the exam. These experiences strongly influenced two of the first principles I sought to incorporate in our educational system when, many years later, I was privileged to become minister responsible for education: remediation and fast-tracking, or Flexible Transfer to Secondary School.

People who teach us and inspire us to become the very best of ourselves deserve a special place. Dame Avis Carrington is one such person. One question that I am sure she was regularly asked in her long career and life is why she wanted to be a teacher. I think her reply might have been "to influence the lives of as many children as possible for the better". And that she did. I am proud and honoured to be one of those persons whose lives she touched.

Barack Obama is aptly quoted in this book as saying: "If you were successful, there is a great teacher somewhere in your life." I endorse this absolutely. Success does not necessarily mean having money or prestigious jobs. As with most of our teachers "back in the day", Dame

Avis never had a degree, as we understand it. But no "degreed" teacher has done more than she—or other teachers of her day—for generations of Barbadian children who have succeeded in all walks of life, not only professionally but quite simply by being good people, evincing confidence, values, ethics, and humanity.

This book illustrates Dame Avis' pride in not only those students who were bright and sharp, but also and especially in those who had to try harder. This is true whether referring to her pupils at St Giles' Primary School, where she taught for twenty-three years, or her wards at Merrivale Preparatory School, the multinational, multicultural, multi-religious school she founded. This school successfully endured for fifty-one years. This fact speaks eloquently to her teaching skills and child-centred philosophy as a teacher. Of course, the children would not have known to articulate that at the time—as I would not have at four years old, when I first met her—but they, as I did, would have known how she made them feel.

Her daughter-in-law Hazel could not have known when she embarked on this biography several years ago, that Dame Avis would be celebrating her centenary while it was being written, and would now be at the blessed age of 102 years. While the secret to a long life remains a mystery, the three answers most Barbadian centenarians provide for their longevity are being physically active; moderate, healthy eating; and a connection to family and the community, including the church.

The characteristic of that last connection is giving rather than receiving. As it says in Acts 20:35 of the Bible: "In everything I did, I showed you that by this kind of hard work we must help the weak, remembering the words the Lord Jesus himself said: 'It is more blessed to give than to receive.'" This is a principle that Dame Avis manifested in a life of purpose. I have had the distinction to be on the receiving end of her belief in this mostly unbelieved beatitude.

To the question of how she wishes to be remembered, Dame Avis offers the modest but powerful reply: "Simply as 'Teacher'. That was what God required of me."

This biography of Dame Avis, or as many of us will forever think of her, Mrs Carrington, provides a tour d'horizon of the evolution of education in Barbados, while it offers a snapshot of Barbadian Black middle-class life in the 20th century. The milestones in her life are the date of her birth, 1918, towards the end of World War I; the riots of 1937; World War II; universal suffrage in Barbados in 1951; the UN Decade of Women, 1976-1985; and the Commission on the Status of Women in 1978 to identify and redress the gender imbalance in Barbados.

I commend *Simply Teacher* to all readers as a contribution to the educational history of Barbados.

I commend it to all Barbadians as a story of one of our builders of Barbados.

Mrs Carrington—thank you, thank you, thank you. We love you.

—Mia Amor Mottley
The Honourable Prime Minister of Barbados

30th June, 2020

Acknowledgements

THE narrative of Dame Avis Carrington started out as a research project that morphed into *Simply Teacher* with the advice and support of several persons.

Thanks to my husband, Ian, for the vision. He pitched the idea for this book and persisted despite her reluctance, "knowing" she would eventually give her consent; and then one day she did. Once invested, Avis gave of her time unsparingly, sharing the memories of her long life and teaching career. Interviews were done over lunch, and there were days when more eating was done than recording, but those were the days when the best stories were told.

Aunt Dan and Pat Byer, provided information about family life in the Inniss household in the Back Ivy. Special thanks to Pat, who shared enthusiastically, as it turned out, from her sick bed. Thanks to Hazel Byer-Horsford for her input after her sister passed away.

I am thankful to those who provided memories of St Giles' Boys' School. I was fortunate to interview the late Irving Wilson, the only remaining contemporary of Avis', before his death in 2015. Glyne Murray, Dr Victor Eastmond, Sir Wesley Hall, Iverton Newton, Lionel Weekes, and Colin Harding shared experiences from the perspective of a student. Mrs Sybil Leacock is also from this earlier period, and shared her experience with the founding of Leacock's Private School in 1948.

I appreciate the enthusiasm and encouragement from teachers, past and present, support staff, parents, students, relatives, volunteers and friends of the school, and for the data they provided through their oral and written testimonies. I especially recognise the contribution from the four staff members who rallied until the closure of the school: Jennifer Holder, Margaret Rock, Antoinette Williams, and Beverly Jones. Miss Jones is worthy of additional mention: she kept in constant contact throughout the years, and her ability to follow a lead and research a story was exceptional. Most of the past students responded to a questionnaire, and others were interviewed, but Mark Skinner submitted anecdotes that captured school life at Merrivale through the eyes of an energetic boy.

I am grateful to those who read the manuscript and provided feedback. Thanks to Marcelle Best, Pamela Brathwaite, Dr Workeley Brathwaite, Beverly Jones, Cynthia Reid, Dr Patricia Saul, and family members Avis, Shelley, Ria, Ian and Ronnie, who also assisted with the photos. Lisa Clarke is in constant contact with 'Teacher' and served as the liaison between the alumni and me; she was the source of some of the pictures featured. While busy with her own studies, she found time to read the manuscript.

Special thanks to Talicia Welcome, the Royal Fidelity National Distinguished Teacher 2018; Dr Patricia Saul; and Lawrence Carrington, Professor Emeritus of Creole Linguistics, University of the West Indies, for their reviews. Lawrence also sourced and provided a wealth of infor-mation about the Trinidadian connection to Avis' life story.

My experience with oversight of writing had been in the form of rig-orous supervision of theses, but this did not prepare me for the nit-pick-ing editor, who was really just doing his job. Carl Moore was the first to edit my early draft; his words of encouragement and enthusiasm spurred me on. My relationship with Robert Edison Sandiford (editor) and Linda M. Deane (design and layout) of ArtsEtc was an education in the transformation of the story of Avis Carrington into *Simply Teacher*. As a novice in the field, the words 'hands held', used to sign off our corre-spondence, reminded me of their unswerving support and patience. I also want to thank my parents, Clayton and Desdemona, for sharing snippets of life from the pre-Independence era, and my mother in par-ticular for her prayers. Thanks to my sister Yvonne and Laurie Blackman whose input was timely in helping to see *Simply Teacher* across the fin-ish line. Thanks for the support.

In the midst of the COVID-19 pandemic, former student of Merriva-le Preparatory School, the Honourable Mia Amor Mottley, Prime Min-ister of Barbados, found the time to write the foreword for this narrative, and I extend my greatest thanks and appreciation.

A heartfelt "Thank you" to all.

Preface

A charming young man with a smart move was responsible for our first meeting. It was a stormy day, and government offices were closed. A promised ride home from work (as it turned out, he had no car) landed me at Shenstone, Pine Road, where his mother, Avis, and I exchanged a quick hello as she busied herself with an early end to the school day. Two years later, on the day that I became her daughter-in-law, Avis spruced up the well-kept garden, transforming it to a delightful backdrop of lush foliage complete with a floral arch where the newlyweds greeted the wedding guests. Ever since that day, our relationship has blossomed into a sweet blend of common interests, mutual respect, and admiration for each other.

"We have a lot in common," she boasts. Our love of gardening takes us on runs to plant nurseries in diverse places, to the annual flower show at Balls Plantation, Open Gardens events, and Agrofest. On several of our outings, she is often asked if I am her daughter. "I have a daughter," she shares quickly, to set the record straight, "but this daughter, my son brought into the family." I also have the pleasure to call her Mum.

We both knew from an early age that teaching was our calling and spent time playing make-believe school with inanimate objects as our pupils. We attended the same secondary school, are both graduates of Erdiston Teachers' Training College, and share a similar philosophy of education, which is all children can learn and school should be a happy place. And as a member of staff at Christ Church Foundation School, I taught a number of Merrivale graduates.

Our passion for teaching and education in general, the special relationship we share, plus the knowledge and skills honed through studies in sociology meant that I was strategically placed to chronicle the life and times of Dame Avisene "Avis" Carrington. *Simply Teacher* traces her journey from timid pupil to teacher, someone who dedicated seventy-four years of her life to teaching and nurturing children: twenty-three in the public service and fifty-one at Merrivale Preparatory School, a private primary school she founded. She celebrated her one-hundredth birthday in September 2018 and rose to national prominence later that year when she received Barbados' highest national award, Dame of St Andrew, for her contribution to early childhood and primary education in Barbados.

When my husband, Ian (that charming man without wheels), pitched the idea for this project, a year would pass before I thought myself capable of writing the story of an education icon. Not that the subject of the biography was keen to cooperate. Avis is a humble person who avoids the limelight. She merely answered her calling, she argued, and could not understand what all the fuss was about. But once she gave the project her blessings, visits to the Carrington home became sessions of storytelling, with snapshots from back in time, laden with nuggets of wisdom and bouts of laughter.

Simply Teacher is not only a celebration of the life of Dame Avis Carrington, it is a narrative of the teaching profession that provides a model for a caring, sharing, supportive, and disciplined yet happy school environment—one in which each child matters.

It spans a period from the early 20th century to the present time; consequently, it is a history of the development of education in Barbados, from limited funding and access, especially for girls in the colony, to government-sponsored education for all in the nation state.

At a time when some writers on the subject argue that teaching does not quite reach the criteria to be classified as a "profession", this narrative renews the pride and status once associated with the job title 'Teacher'.

Mum, you dedicated your heart and soul to teaching. Your love for children and your passion and commitment to their education and wellbeing continue to inspire.

—Hazel Lindo-Carrington
Bridgetown, Barbados

Simply Teacher

ONE

"A task ever dear to my heart, a task that I firmly believe that God required of me...." —Avis Carrington, 1999

Avis receiving Barbados' highest national honour, Dame of St. Andrew, on Independence Day, 30 November, 2018.

A Divine Calling

IT was the 30th of November and Barbadians painted Kensington Oval a collage of ultramarine and gold in celebration of the 52nd anniversary of the nation. Dark gloomy clouds rained on the parade but failed to alter the precision and poise of the pageantry or dampen the enthusiasm of the spectators who clapped and cheered on the uniformed troops who braved the persistent showers. Momentarily, droplets opted to stay suspended in the clouds and the sun peeked out as if in acknowledgement of her accomplishment.

At 100 years old, Avisene Carrington was the first centenarian among the honourees in the Barbados National Independence Honours of 2018. Fittingly, head boys and head girls from all primary and secondary schools received leadership badges, a first, on the day that she received the highest class of award for her contribution to early childhood and primary education in Barbados.

But how did this self-confessed hater of school grow to embrace education, make teaching children her life's passion, and go on to found a school that would earn her the country's highest national award?

Avis, as she preferred to be called, had a passion for teaching from an early age. Her calling had its origin in a divine plan that kept her in school for eighty-seven years. She disliked school. It was 1920s Barbados and teaching strategies were limited to chalk, talk, reprimands and flogging. Her earliest memories are of difficult sums to solve, hard words to spell, the glare of a stern teacher, and children trembling in fear of the strap. A timid child could not cope in this setting, and cope Avis did not. She was afraid of her teachers, which heightened her discomfort and slowed her progress.

She particularly disliked when she was compared to Dan, who was considered the bright one in the family. Teachers assumed she would follow in her older sister's footsteps and never failed to remind her. "Why are you not like your sister?" they often asked and followed the question with, "You will grow up to be nothing but a washerwoman." If this was intended to improve her performance, it failed utterly. The pressure of this strategy only added to her anxiety.

But after stumbling at the elementary level, Avis found her stride and emerged from her sister's shadow. Teachers at the secondary level were kind and caring and helped her to discover her academic potential. She grew from being timid and withdrawn, into a confident and engaged student; it was this transformation that inspired her love of teaching and later in a speech, Avis would describe it as:

"A task ever dear to my heart, a task that I firmly believe that God required of me."

Opportunities for women were limited to nursing, sewing and teaching. Avis did not see herself as a nurse, and fear of being lashed for a faulty stitch lingered from her school days, limiting her dress-making skills to the basics. But this was not simply a process of elimination; Avis loved children and was naturally drawn to teaching. Six weeks after graduating from secondary school, she became the first female teacher at St Giles' Boys' School, one of the most outstanding elementary schools of the day.

The headmaster Charles Wilkinson "Wilkie" Cumberbatch was a

visionary and mentor who excelled in his quest to prepare boys for entry into the island's prestigious secondary schools. Under his guidance, eighteen-year old Avis would grow to become an exceptional teacher. However, she would depart from the traditional harsh, rigid approach to teaching and discipline and develop a safe and happy space for children, especially those who needed additional tuition and support.

But her career in the public service was merely the beginning of her teaching legacy. As a young wife and mother, Avis was faced with the choice of home-schooling her three-year-old son Ian, or continuing in her post, and she made a decision, truly bold for the time. In September 1959, she opened her heart and her home to three children; Ian made four. This playgroup which met in the dining room for half a day each weekday, mushroomed into Merrivale Preparatory School.

At its peak in the 1970s, the school had a roll of over 220 students. Avis maintained a focus on academic excellence, while ensuring Merrivale was disciplined without being harsh, and most importantly, the children were "happy." This was one of the tenets on which the school stood. It defined the ethos and was reflected in the name of the school. Merrivale coexisted with the Carrington home in an inextricable bond that lasted fifty-one years, and brought the educator national acclaim.

In her life span, Avis evolved from a timid elementary school girl to become a confident high school graduate and an outstanding teacher at a leading elementary school. She became the founder of what would become a leading private preparatory school. To her teaching colleagues in her early years she was "Miss Inniss," and in 1947 she married Vere Carrington and took his name. To her staff at Merrivale she was "Mrs Carrington" and to her students wherever she served she was "Teacher." To her children she was "Mum," "A-A" to her nieces and "Gran" to her grandchildren. On November 30, 2018, Avis Carrington received Barbados' highest national award, and thereafter would be referred to as "Dame."

TWO

"Train up a child in the way he should go: and when he is old, he shall not depart from it." —Proverbs 22:6

The village in the Back Ivy, St Michael, where Avis spent her childhood. Nik's Discount Supermarket now occupies the corner lot formerly owned by the Innisses.

Growing up Inniss

THE Innisses were the "cream" of the Back Ivy, the most northerly of intersecting gaps and lanes that made up the larger area known as the Ivy. The village was situated towards the southern end of the parish of St Michael, approximately two miles outside of Bridgetown, the capital city of Barbados, an island which sits in the Atlantic Ocean, and is the most easterly of a chain of islands in the Caribbean Sea.

Prominent families lived on the main road. Noted educator Florence Springer, for whom Springer Memorial School is named, and her nephew Hugh Springer, later Sir Hugh, who became a National Hero and the third native Governor General of Barbados, lived on Government Hill. Just off this main road, the Tudors owned the Lincoln Bus Company and operated a fleet of buses before there was a public transportation system. Tudor's Funeral Home owned by the same family was founded in 1894, and still operates from the same location in the Ivy.

Life among the majority black population in the village was characterised by a laid-back sense of contentment despite the high unemployment and a life of poverty. Persons fortunate enough to find work were mostly artisans, domestics and agricultural labourers.

Children roamed the village in oversized hand-me-downs, clothing passed from older siblings or given by the 'mistress' who employed their mothers. Most of the children went bare-footed, even to school; and those who owned this rare commodity saved them for church, as a sign of reverence.

The Innisses were exceptions. Both Robert Inniss, known as Bob by his close friends and Mr Inniss by his neighbours, and his wife Beatrice, had a seventh-standard education, the highest level of elementary education available, and held high status jobs for the times. Mr Inniss was employed by the Barbados Light Railway Company Limited as a conductor on the island's sole train from Bridgetown, the capital in St Michael, to Belleplaine in St Andrew. Mr Inniss was a well-spoken man, and unlike most in the village who spoke Bajan dialect, he conversed as an equal with the owners of plantations and their overseers in Standard English. This distinction brought him, and by extension the whole family much status in the community.

Beatrice came from a family of teachers but opted for nursing because of her desire to provide care to the sick. She worked on the Eye Ward at Barbados General Hospital located in a separate building at the western end of Jemmotts Lane. The Queen Elizabeth Hospital, at the corner of River Road and Martindale's Road, replaced the old facility in 1964. As was customary then, she was forced to give up her job once she became a wife and mother.

The family owned a bluish grey gabled-roofed wooden house with white trim which sat on a sprawling corner lot now occupied by Nik's Discount Supermarket. Obliquely opposite and across the street stood Blenheim Plantation, now the home of the National Sports Council (NSC).

A three-tiered step at the front of the house led to a gated entrance which opened into an enclosed porch. This was kept cool by long jalousie windows propped up with long wooden sticks. There was a large living and dining area and a comfortable kitchen where Miss Inniss enjoyed preparing meals for the family.

The availability of some amenities set the Inniss family apart from their neighbours. While it was common place for the villagers to gather at the standpipe to fetch water and catch up on the latest gossip, the Inniss home was equipped with running water. This was considered a luxury in those days. Electricity was not yet available, and households depended on light provided by kerosene lamps and lanterns. The lamps with their decorative glass chimneys, some stating "Home Sweet Home," others "God Bless our Home," were strategically placed on a table or mantle. The sturdier lanterns with an enclosed flame were portable and reserved for use outdoors.

Centrally located in the village was "Miss Small shop," where most of the neighbours bought groceries; but Robert Inniss ordered his goods from merchants in Bridgetown, only relying on the corner shop for smaller items which were purchased by the housekeeper. There was no refrigerator; ice was bought from a cart that made weekly trips through the area. It was stored in an ice chest which also served to refrigerate perishable food.

These privileges were never flaunted. A Christian family, the Innisses were known for their humility and generosity, and readily shared with their neighbours. The family raised livestock, and the property had an abundance of fruit trees with a delightful mix of flowering shrubs and herbaceous plants. They grew a variety of vegetables and ground provisions which provided food for many of the villagers, including the local petty thief, to keep him out of trouble.

Mrs Inniss was "Godma" to the children, even when formal requests had not been made by their parents. She became "Mama" and her husband "Papa" when they adopted their first daughter Erdine before they had children of their own. Constance, called Dan, was the first, born on 29 May, 1916.

This was the home in which Avisene "Avis" Caesaretta Inniss, was born on Tuesday, 17 September, 1918. Avis and her siblings had everything they needed, and life at home was comfortable and happy. Playing with the neighbours' children was allowed but the girls had no close friends in the village. Papa did not approve. Mama was a woman of faith; she was generous and shared with those who were needy, and her home was a refuge for the children of friends and family alike.

May Nicholls was taken in when her father died, allowing her mother to train for a career in nursing. Catherine Goring, called "Baby," because she was the last of seven Goring children, was Mrs Inniss' actual goddaughter. Louis Thorne was an older cousin from St Philip. When he won a scholarship to Harrison College, the Back Ivy residence became his weekday home because of its proximity to the school. Cousin Millie Inniss died of tuberculosis; even though it was a very contagious disease which caused her isolation from family members, Mrs Inniss cared for her until her death.

The family worshipped at St Barnabas Anglican Church in St Michael, where a rented pew was reserved for them. The matriarch was devout; she never missed church except for bad weather. On such occasions, the children gathered in the living room at eleven o'clock sharp for Sunday worship. Mama's evangelical enthusiasm was not always shared by the children, especially Avis. They attended the Sunday morning service at the family church, usually a two-hour affair. After a quick meal they were sent off to Sunday School at Belmont Methodist Church which started at 3 p.m. and lasted for an hour and a half. The church was near to the family home and their mother thought it fitting to have the children further steeped in Christian doctrine, even though from a different denomination. Avis and her siblings participated in the singing and reciting of poems for various programmes. Dramatic presentations came later as these were once frowned upon.

Avis and her siblings had a strict upbringing. Her father had a stern disposition and never interacted with children in a playful way, until his first grandchild Pat arrived and softened him. He was guided by the maxim that "Children should be seen and not heard." His mates would drop by the house and they would discuss the issues of the day. Even as a teenager, Avis was excluded and paid little attention, until the time there was a sense of urgency in their tone. Not long after, Avis got ready for her weekly walk to the Barbados Public Library but never made it into Bridgetown. She was on her way when her neighbour Adelle called out.

"Where are you going?"
"To the library," Avis replied.
"You cannot go today; I heard there is shooting in town."

It was the 26th of July, the first day of the 1937 Labour Rebellion also known as the Bridgetown Riots. Avis had been teaching for almost a year when words of protest and potential trouble became central to the conversation in the home, mainly between her father and his friends. The uprising impacted the social life in the colony, resulting in historic political reforms.

Mr Inniss was a dignified gentleman and his wife was a fine example of poise and grace, and they expected nothing less than ladylike behaviour from the children. Papa monitored their activities and frowned upon anything that did not reach his high standards. They could play in front of the house, but only for short periods, looking on with envy as boys roamed free all over the neighbourhood, only with a caution to stay out of "the hot broiling sun." The girls dared not venture beyond boundaries that were stated though unmarked. This kept them within range so Papa could keep his eyes on their activities.

Despite these restrictions, the girls spent time playing games, with other children, "whatever took their fancy," hands clapping and feet tapping along to rhythmic songs with catchy lyrics. Those that included a jiggle of the hips were not allowed. Skipping was a favourite. Chanting rhymes like "I doan want nuh chip up potatoes, gie me me dumplings whole," two persons held either end of a long rope and swung it while a third player jumped over on the down swing. The girls enjoyed racing against each and later Avis would participate in athletics at secondary school.

In some games two teams competed against each other. In rounders, a small ball was pitched and struck by the hitter who ran around four stones arranged in the form of a large square. If the ball was thrown back to the starting point while the hitter was not at a base, then the player was given out. Hopscotch tested accuracy and balance, as squares on a grid were won and used to restrict the movement of opponents.

The full moon provided the right mood for an occasional late night of storytelling or a game of hide-and-seek in its soft light. On some evenings, the mobile cinema—a screen and projector on wheels—came to the village and curious children, accompanied by their parents, flocked around to watch the educational clips mixed in with light-hearted comedy; this the Inniss girls overheard from others as Papa never allowed them to attend. On the fifth of November every year, until November 1966 when the holiday was abolished, the Innisses celebrated Guy Fawkes Day with fireworks and conkies, a cornmeal treat with pumpkin, coconut, and sweet potato steamed in a banana leaf. Early morning walks were for adults only. The neighbours met at 5 o'clock and set off on a route that varied daily.

Erdine grew into a much sought-after seamstress after starting her craft by practising on her dolls, a favourite way to pass the time indoors. The girls took this game to a new level when weddings were held in their little dollhouses. Erdine made the fancy outfits for the occasion, and even sold some of her designs to the other girls. She would eventually "turn out" many brides, as Barbadians say, including her sister Avis.

Other indoor games were pick-ups, in which stones were gathered and thrown a short distance into the air and then caught on the back of the hand. This was similar to jacks, played with a small ball and a set of six-pronged metal pieces that gave the game its name. The jacks were scattered, the ball was thrown into the air, and the pieces were retrieved, in ones, then twos, increasing with each round as the game progressed. The ball had to be caught after the first bounce or play was passed to the next player.

None of the children had assigned chores, but Erdine and Dan didn't mind helping out in the kitchen as an extension of their indoor play. Mama was an excellent cook and tried recipes from a collection of cookbooks. Even though she had help, she enjoyed cooking and passed these skills on to the older girls, who grew to enjoy entertaining and preparing meals for big family gatherings. Avis had no interest in things culinary but developed a love for cake-making when kitchen appliances were modernised. The brick oven, made of fireproof brick and heated with coals, was neither pleasant nor an easy undertaking for a teenager. Of all the games at her disposal, playing school was Avis' favourite. While she mimicked her teachers by being stern and even using a strap, she was kinder to the classroom of dolls and empty bottles that were her students.

Avis and Erdine, tomboys by their own admission, longed for the outdoors. They would wander into the woods at Blenheim and climb trees, throw stones and pick grasses that Erdine would then use for basket weaving. Pitching marbles, playing with a roller (the steel rim of a bicycle wheel, usually guided by a stick) or shooting a gutter-perk (a slingshot or catapult made of a V-shaped twig and used for hunting birds) were all meant for boys and were clearly off-limits. Their sister Dan, dubbed the bookworm by Avis, was the studious one and Papa's favourite; she preferred the indoors. Her only outdoor activity was a fun day she planned for the children of the village. What a delight if the cart selling "frozen joy," a lolly on a stick, passed through the village on fun day.

Surprisingly, Papa broke with tradition when he allowed the girls to play cricket. He was an avid fan and bought them caps and a bat and taught them how to play the game. Avis never caught on. She was constantly reminded that she was not "holding the bat right," and was afraid to fail and disappoint her father. Even as an adult she never developed a love for the game, she preferred football; and when the West Indies cricket team celebrated its dominance in the world, Avis showed little interest.

If her father had been able to read her mind, he would have understood how much she longed to join her adventurous playmates who always seemed to be having more fun. But she knew her father; he would never allow her deepest desire, to feel the thrill of speeding along on a bicycle with the wind blowing against her face. Riding was unladylike, she was told, but never understood. Was the bicycle not called a "lady's wheel?"

Avis soon stumbled upon the opportunity to fulfil her wish. Arthur Byer, Robert Inniss' nephew, was a frequent visitor to his uncle's home. He rode his bicycle from St George to the Back Ivy and back, except on those occasions when it rained, and the bicycle was left overnight. On the morning after, Arthur's bicycle was leaning against the house, glossy black with gold stripes accentuating the frame and shiny silver spokes radiating from the centre of each wheel. She could not contain her excitement and immediately solicited help.

Erdine's retiring disposition masked her tenacity and daring. A threat of lashes did not deter her from getting home late from school, if it meant stopping by a new shop with novelty sweets. Avis in tow with tears streaming down her cheek would try to dissuade her; all the while she was torn between going straight home with Dan, or choosing to follow Erdine, knowing there would be consequences.

"Erdine and I got a lot of lashes," Avis confessed.

With Erdine at her side the pair planned to venture out on a cycling spree, but neither of the girls could ride. This was not seen as a deterrent; rather, the girls dismissed this as a minor problem. The more adventurous Erdine mounted the bike while Avis held it firmly against a protruding rock-face that was used as a prop. After struggling to find her balance, she achieved some stability, and started to pedal, gingerly at first, but gaining momentum and confidence with every push of the pedal.

These early attempts were interrupted by near misses, a few falls, and some scratches; these were on the poor bike. A passer-by observed the spectacle. Had they been the owners, he probably reasoned, they would have treated it with greater care. "I wonder who that bicycle belong to," he muttered to himself. "Dem must be thief it." The girls had taken the bike without permission and were taking full advantage to achieve the goal they had set themselves. They were determined and persisted until the bike cooperated, and they achieved something approximating mastery.

Avis and her sister Erdine advanced quickly. From a wobbly start on that first day, they were soon making steady, effortless sprints and forgetting that riding was prohibited. Until one day Avis was racing, first one way and then the other on the unpaved road in front of the house, when she barely noticed the frantic gestures of her sister. As she reduced her speed, the reason for the hysterics became apparent. There was Papa standing stoically on the front porch of the house, gazing into the distance, maybe for his occasional check on the girls.

Now a competent rider, Avis chose not to retreat. Instead, she flattened her back and lowered her head, the wind flowing easily over her crouched body. Now pedalling hard and gaining speed, she whizzed past the house before her father's failing eyes could focus. Robert Inniss was proud of his girls; they always obeyed the rules and only indulged in behaviours that met with his approval, but this was only as far as he could see.

Surprisingly, kite-flying, another pastime considered for boys only, was allowed. The girls looked forward to Easter when a kaleidoscope of geometric patterns of thin translucent paper pasted on frames of wood, with tails of knotted pieces of colourful fabric took to the sky. Papa always got the girls a kite at Easter; these were always made by someone in the village, and never sold. Once the kite was airborne, they took turns holding the cord which kept it suspended, daring to let it soar to new heights or carefully controlling its range. The more adventurous would tug this way then that, teasing the kite into a display of twirls; the angry "bull" or hummer, a piece of tissue paper suspended from the arched hood ("round head") of the kite buzzing angrily in response to every pull. Then reversing the action gradually, the kite would resume a steady calm, or not.

The girls were cautious. They knew that a gust of wind could cause a loss of lift; the kite could nosedive into the ground, and a smile could easily morph into a frown. Yet these were the exact conditions under which Avis lost control of the kite. She pulled and pulled on the string and watched sadly as the stubborn kite snaked its way to the ground, landing in a tangled mess inside a distant yard. While Erdine played the role of lookout, Avis ventured in to retrieve it, but before she could make her escape, she was nipped by a playful dog. The barely visible scratch was kept a secret from her parents. In her enthusiasm to retrieve the kite, she had wandered into forbidden territory.

The girls were at their best when attending the annual Agricultural and Industrial Exhibition in Queen's Park, a five-minute walk east of Bridgetown; and Papa specially rented a car for the occasion. The open-air show and competition of the best livestock and produce featured cows, pigs, sheep, goats and pigeons, and craftsmen and women displayed their handiwork. It was also a fashion fest that attracted large numbers of visitors dressed in their Sunday-best, clothing worn on special occasions. Ladies showed off their Leghorn hats made of plaited straw, with wide brims and decorated with velvet ribbon and flowers. The men wore stylish felt hats with pinched crowns and brims.

The Royal Barbados Police Force Band promenade, an open-air concert performed in the bandstand in the park, was the only other event that was comparable, and it is still held annually at the same venue. Every Christmas morning, folks stroll leisurely throughout the grounds; some showing off clothing bought specially for the occasion, while others listen attentively or sway to the music of the orchestra.

Beatrice was Robert's second wife and much younger. She was tall and stately and always a picture of elegance in her attire, with her beaming daughters following close behind in matching outfits. Mr Inniss chose the finest fabrics and had their clothes sewn by the top seamstress in the area. They featured can-cans, an under garment made of stiff layers of net that added flounce to the garment. The outfits were accessorised with colour-coordinated ribbons to decorate their slightly straightened hair; Papa did not approve of the "ironing comb"; but Mama indulged the girls making sure to leave enough curl so that it would not attract Papa's attention. The attire was not complete without new shoes with shiny buckles and cute little pocketbooks. Neighbours gathered in the street with glances of approval as the dapperly dressed head of the household proudly escorted the family.

Avis marvelled at her mother's dedication, from the rearing of the livestock to the preparation of the animals for the event; only the best animals were entered for awards. This tradition was passed on from the Inniss brothers and enthusiastically embraced by Mrs Inniss. It was considered a privilege to attend, but many parents could not afford to send their children to the paid event. Instead, the neighbourhood children beamed with excitement as they gathered to watch the animals as they were carted off to Queen's Park to be paraded. This was the closest they got to the exhibition, but celebrated when word reached the village that the Innisses had won for "best animal on show."

The other animals suffered a different fate; their demise came in the dim light of "fore-day" morning. With sharpened tools and a long, twisted rope wrapped around his shoulder, and cries of "What's fat, what's fat," the village butcher traversed the neighbourhood advertising his services in advance of the kill. Early Saturday morning, the piercing squeals of a pig signalled that the mission had been accomplished, and neighbours who had "engaged the pork" had parcels of meat wrapped in brown paper delivered to their homes.

One young boy was fond of the livestock and was always present to watch the finest animals on their way to be exhibited. But this was new to him, and he could not rest until he had the rumour verified.

"Dah is true dat de pig get kill?" he enquired of Avis. When the fate of his favourite boar was confirmed, he asked with genuine concern:

"So wuh he do?"

*

It was a Monday bank-holiday, the day of the church outing, and picnic baskets were packed to capacity. The pork, chicken and the eggs for baking came from animals bred by the Innisses, and the vegetables and the limes for the lemonade were grown in their garden. Every Easter the girls joined their father on the train as he performed his duties as conductor, while they enjoyed the ride on the way to visit their uncle James Inniss.

James, whom the girls called Uncle Jim, was a merchant and owned a grocery store and haberdashery. He was the only black man in his area who owned a car. The girls were picked up from Three Houses station which was a few miles away from his home in Blades Hill, St Philip. The highlight of their stay was "despatching" customers with their purchases of buttons, fancy ribbon and thread.

But today the destination was further along the route, to Bathsheba in the parish of St Joseph. The Barbados Railway transported passengers and freight from 1883 to 1937 on the line that ran from Bridgetown in the west to its final stop, Belleplaine, in St Andrew on the eastern coast of the island. The church folk dressed up in brightly coloured bank-holiday clothing, specially made for the occasion. The crowd of picnickers assembled at Rouen, the second station out of Bridgetown, for the long ride. They packed themselves into the "Penny Train," an open carriage aimed at the less affluent in society and specially used for the occasion. As the ride continued across country, folk songs, lively choruses, loud chatter, and bouts of laughter kept the mood light and cheerful.

Mr Inniss never abandoned thoughts of propriety and was never too busy conducting to keep an eye on his daughters. They sat in the more prestigious closed carriage, away from what their father saw as vulgar behaviour; but for Avis and her sisters, this was yet another occasion when other children seemed to be having more fun. They chatted in barely audible whispers, creating their own muffled amusement.

One thing they shared with their fellow travellers was their enjoyment of the scenic ride. From Rouen, the train continued on through the St George Valley, to Three Houses and then Bushy Park in St Philip before turning left onto the scenic east coast with its view of the vast Atlantic Ocean and the smell of the sea on the edge of the north east trade winds. After two more stops, one at Bath and the other at Martin's Bay, the hungry travellers finally disembarked at Bathsheba.

At the picnic site, brightly patterned tins lost their covers to reveal tightly packed layers of "pudding," a yellow cake made of butter, eggs, sugar and flour; and corned beef sandwiches. But it was Mrs Inniss' basket, packed with peas and rice, baked pork and beef stew that attracted the crowd. Hefty servings of food were washed down with an "enamel cup" of lemonade or mauby. Small groups wandered off

Some explored the rugged terrain, while others chose a sea bath in one of the safe pools away from the raging tide.

Papa always kept a close eye on his daughters. Dan was always eager to please while Avis and her co-conspirator Erdine were constantly plotting how they could escape his persistent vigilance. In contrast to the demands he made, Papa was not harsh with punishment; his firm demeanour and high expectations kept the girls in check. He was totally against flogging children; it was Mama who used spanking, with a mix of alternative methods like the loss of a privilege. Even though her parents were strict and her father stern in his disposition, they were "kind, passionate and caring." Later Avis would have to balance the role of disciplinarian with that of a loving teacher.

THREE

"If you were successful...There was a great teacher somewhere in your life." —Barack Obama

Simply Teacher: The Life of Avis Carrington

Avis and her sisters Erdine and Dan attended Belmont Girls' School (now Belmont Primary) at Odessa Drive, My Lord's Hill.

School Days

HAPPY carefree days ended for Avis when she started elementary school at age five. The only ease came on weekends and during school vacations that she hoped would never end. Avis was taunted by her teachers, while her sister Dan, the "bright one" and Papa's favourite, won their admiration. As if to compensate, Avis sought out the bravery and daring of her sister Erdine, they would become best friends. She also benefitted from the comfort of an understanding and compassionate mother. The two would develop a close bond that would last until her mother passed away.

Avis attended the Belmont Girls' School which was the designated school for girls in the surrounding areas. It was founded as an infant school by the Methodist Church in 1894 and catered primarily to girls. Single-sex infant schools were often coeducational and though intended for children between five and eight, older students were sometimes enrolled. The Anglican Church, the established church of Barbados, sided with the planters in their bid to restrict the formal education of slaves, providing the opportunity for other denominations to intervene. Despite persecution, the Methodist Church persisted in its dissent of this position and earned a place in the history of education in the region. The Anglican Church redeemed itself when the British Government appointed William Coleridge, Bishop of Barbados in 1824. He established schools for coloureds, utilising chapels, not only as places of worship, but also for schooling.

By the time Avis attended elementary school in 1923, the school's wooden structure had already been moved from its earlier location in the churchyard of the Belmont Methodist Church to its present site at Odessa McClean Drive, further east along My Lord's Hill. The schoolhouse had an open plan typical of schoolhouses of the day. Classes occupied the hall and were separated only by the strategic positioning of black boards. The office of the headmistress was a raised area at the front, where she had a panoramic view of the staff and student body.

Avis found elementary school boring and unfriendly, and the teachers were intimidating. Emphasis was placed primarily on arithmetic and English, the two subjects that were tested for promotion. Rote learning and drill were the methods used to teach at a time when children were treated as empty vessels to be filled with knowledge. Spelling, and the reciting of the times-tables, also called multiplication tables, to near perfection, were popular methods of assessment. Avis cowered in fear of the dreaded dictation and later she vowed to never use it in her teaching methods. Pupils trembled as they attempted to solve mathematical problems on the spot, without the benefit of pencil and slate, in what was dubbed "mental arithmetic." Every incorrect answer would earn the frightened child a lash. The mass training of teachers, which came with the founding of Erdiston Teachers' Training College in 1948, was still in the future; so too was a broader awareness of obstacles that some students faced.

Robert Inniss was determined to give his daughters a secondary education, at a time when access for females to that level was limited; and furthermore, it would be costly to pay school fees for three girls.

This situation changed when he secured funding for one of the girls. Dan was a sickly child and spent time indoors with her books. Unlike Avis, who showed little interest when Erdine shared her school work, she was keen to learn from her older sister. This advanced her academic performance and she stood out among her peers.

Dan was in standard two when her teacher noticed that she was often distracted by something outside of her class. This offence would certainly have resulted in a flogging, but she was spared after an investigation revealed that after completing her tasks, she would solve the arithmetic problems intended for standard three pupils in the adjacent class. The discovery of this talented child was promptly brought to the attention of the headmistress, and she was chosen to prepare for the Primary to First Grade Scholarship. If successful, she would attend Queen's College, the only first-grade school for girls in the colony.

The designations first-grade and second-grade to describe secondary schools in Barbados were recommendations of the Mitchinson Commission of 1875.

These schools differed in duration of schooling, curriculum content and available funding, and from inception, a strong bias existed in favour of upper-class boys for the limited places they offered. By 1900, eight Government-funded schools provided secondary education: two of the first-grade schools, Harrison College and The Lodge School, and four second-grade schools: Combermere School, The Coleridge School, The Parry School, and The Alleyne School, were for boys. Only two schools, Alexandra School, second-grade and Queen's College, first-grade were for girls.

Papa often boasted about Dan's academic prowess to family and friends, and he was determined to see her pass the scholarship exam. The family invested much time and funds in her preparation. Mama spent hours coaching her daughter, and the headmistress, Mrs Emily Lewis was paid for additional lessons. The investment in Dan paid off in 1927 when she won the scholarship and gained entry to the prestigious Queen's College, a year after she took the first exam.

Dan successfully completed the exam in 1926 but watched sadly as another student was awarded. It was rumoured that race may have been a factor. The official story was that the recipient was more deserving because she had written a tougher exam; these were not yet regulated or standardised. The score on the exam was not transferable and Dan was forced to rewrite the exam the following year.

Dan would enter the teaching service at the elementary level and taught at Belmont Primary School before furthering her education. She earned a Bachelor of Arts degree and completed a teacher training programme at the University of London. She taught at St Michael's Girls' School and tutored at Erdiston Teachers' Training College before returning to St Michael's Girls' School where she was appointed headmistress and served until her retirement in 1976.

Throughout their elementary school days, Avis and Erdine were overshadowed by their studious sister Dan, who excelled academically; but with funding for her education secured, Robert Inniss could turn his attention to secondary education for his other two daughters. The girls were fortunate. In some homes, boys were educated beyond elementary level while their sisters were not. And in others, a bright child could be singled out and fed a more nutritious diet, like the single egg from the chicken coop, or be the recipient of text books while other siblings went without.

The founding of St Michael's Girls' School as a second-grade school in 1928 by the St Michael Vestry was timely, and Erdine and Avis would attend as fee-paying students. The Vestry was part of a system of local government that managed parochial issues, including the provision of scholarships and exhibitions to assist the poor with financial aid. Erdine was enrolled at St Michael's Girls' School in its first year. She was gifted with her hands and left school to pursue her interest in sewing.

She became a top seamstress in the area and was known for her bridal designs.

Wherever there was a wedding, villagers would walk long distances—there were no buses—just to find fault with the bride. "Wuh she cudda stan home," or "She pass; wunnah cahn say a ting," were words spoken when the bridal gown met or did not meet with the approval of the critics. It was this kind of informal advertising that expanded Erdine's business. Her staff of uniformed assistants started at ten in the morning and worked until five in the evening. The holiday period was especially busy with demands for new clothes for the Agricultural Exhibition and Christmas morning in Queen's Park. Erdine also taught Domestic Science and Handicraft at the House Craft Centre, a school for adult education, and supplied the Women's Self Help with crocheted, embroidered, knitted, plaited, tatted, and woven items for sale.

Avis followed her sister Erdine two years later. The fees were set at $5 per term for prep and $8 beyond that level, but by the time Avis graduated the fees had risen to $21 per term paid in Barbadian currency. These banknotes were issued by commercial banks in the 1920s and 1930s and by the Government of Barbados in the 1940s. The payment of fees kept the masses away from school, especially at the secondary level, until the founding of the Secondary Modern School.

With the establishment of Secondary Modern Schools, later called Comprehensive Schools, more places became available at the secondary level, but boys continued to be favoured with greater access to a grammar school education. Comprehensive schools provided instruction that was practical, and students were not expected to attend university. They were different from the first-grade and second-grade schools which were based on the British model of grammar schools which offered students an academic curriculum that prepared them for entry to higher education.

The first two Secondary Modern schools were, St Leonard's Boys' and St Leonard's Girls', opened in 1952; two coeducational schools followed in 1955, Princess Margaret School and West St Joseph Secondary Modern School, later renamed the Grantley Adams Memorial School. Fees were not paid at these schools from inception, but payment for a grammar school education remained a feature of secondary education in Barbados until its abolition in 1962. To change the perception of comprehensive schools, each secondary school in Barbados is designated a Government Secondary School; but the public's view of the status of these schools remained.

*

In Avis' early school life, limited training and scarce resources had a negative impact on the quality of instruction she received and hindered her progress. But at St Michael's Girls' School "great teachers" saw her potential and transformed her school life. Miss Lucy Brown, the headmistress, was a proponent of student-centred learning, a strategy that focuses on students and their individual needs. The time had come for Avis' redemption.

During Miss Brown's tenure, school fees were lowered, and government exhibitions and bursaries made available, allowing more students to attend school. She loved her students and allowed them the use of her personal collection of books. Under her headship, the house system was introduced to stimulate interest in sports and to encourage student participation. The four houses were named after queens of England and identified by colours: Ann, yellow; Boadicea, blue; Elizabeth, purple; and Victoria, red.

Avis' love of the outdoors continued into secondary school. There was no inter-school sports meet; instead, each school held its own event with competing houses or sets. Avis successfully represented Elizabeth House in netball and athletics. Her favourite event was sprinting, and she always placed in the top three, winning the approval of the cheering crowd. She had a love for guiding, but without Papa's approval she looked on while others joined the company.

Nella Taitt, one of the earliest pioneers was one of Avis' teachers. When she accepted a post at the St Michael's School, she closed the private school she founded in Fairchild Street and brought forty students to the newly established school. Miss Thorne had a warm personality and was Avis' favourite teacher. She developed caring relationships with her students, offering them free tuition at her home at Tyrol Cot in Codrington Hill, St Michael. Miss Thorne later became Lady Grace Adams, wife of Sir Grantley Adams, the first Premier of Barbados and mother of Jon Michael Geoffrey Manningham Adams, better known as "Tom," the country's second Prime Minister. Tyrol Cot Heritage Village is now a museum which features the family home, with its antique furniture and memorabilia, chattel houses and a rum-shop.

At age sixteen, Avis completed the Junior Cambridge Certificate, with passes in English, algebra, arithmetic, geometry, literature, history, geography, religious knowledge and French. Unlike today when students receive a certificate for each subject passed, Avis required passes in five subjects to qualify for a single certificate. Papa thought Avis was old enough to seek employment, and with the increase in student enrolment at the elementary level, she would secure a post in the teaching service. But Mama was firm in her belief that she should spend an additional two years and complete the Senior Cambridge Certificate, later called O level (Ordinary level). An Advanced Level certificate (A-Level) was also offered by the examining body.

Certification in Barbados was administered by the University of Cambridge and the University of London until the Caribbean Examinations Council was established in 1972 and became the examining body for the region. The first exams, the Caribbean Secondary Examination Certificate (CSEC), equivalent to the O level, were set in 1979 in five subjects. Among the range of certification developed to meet the needs of its sixteen participating countries is the Caribbean Advanced Proficiency Examination (CAPE), the equivalent of the Advanced Level certificate.

At a time when the brightest fourteen-year-old boys were recruited to teach at the elementary level, eighteen-year old Avis with the junior and senior Cambridge certification was more than qualified for a career in teaching.

FOUR

*"In a completely rational society,
the best of us would be teachers and the rest of us
would have to settle for something less."* —Lee Iacocca

Simply Teacher: The Life of Avis Carrington

In 1936, Avis Inniss became an honorary teacher at St Giles'
Boys' School, now St Giles' Primary School.

Avis' Dream Job

A S a novice in her field, Avis Inniss knew little about the teaching profession. As a pupil at elementary school, she witnessed teaching at its most basic level. Teachers taught, and when outcomes fell below expectations, they resorted to harsh reprimands and punishment. But over the span of her teaching career, through mentoring, formal training and her own instincts, she would learn the role of the teacher, hone her teaching skills and develop a philosophy of teaching and learning that would define the school she founded.

The primary role of the teacher is to impart knowledge, and to use assessment tools to determine if students understand the concepts. But this is only part of what teachers do. Teachers are charged with the responsibility of identifying learning objectives, or outcomes for each lesson taught. These are achieved by using teaching strategies that should be compatible with the learning style of each child. Competent teachers vary their methods to achieve this objective.

The experienced teacher ensures that students reach beyond basic rote learning and recall to comprehension, practical applications of the knowledge they acquire, levels of analysis and evaluation. The best lessons include strategies that allow students to express feelings and develop values.

Teachers immediately assume the status of "role model," second only to parents. Their conduct becomes part of the "hidden curriculum," lessons that are passed on to students even when not intended. They manage the classroom effectively, balancing discipline with praise, building character, developing confidence and enhancing self-esteem. Compassionate teachers build lasting relationships of trust with students and their parents that extend beyond school and into homes. Great teachers inspire students to develop a lifelong love of learning.

*

Avis Inniss started her teaching career at St Giles' Boys' School in 1936. She was among the graduates who were assigned to elementary schools as honorary teachers who worked without remuneration. The period before receiving a salary was at the discretion of the headteacher; the time varied from school to school and could last for several years. Her sister Constance Inniss (Dan) taught at Belmont Girls' School for two years and to quote her, "for not one cent." Fortunately for Avis, Mr Wilkie Cumberbatch the headmaster at St Giles' Boys' School saw something special in her. After serving for one year, the young Miss Inniss received her first salary. She saw the delay as a time to satisfy "the powers that be" that the recruits were ready to move on to paid status.

Teachers were also recruited from the student body. The brightest fourteen-year-old boys, each armed with a certificate of character from his minister-of-the-gospel, taught younger students under the guidance of a master in what was called the Teacher-Pupil system. Unlike the honorary teachers, the boys were paid a small stipend.

The history of the school includes the headship of Fitzherbert Alleyne Breedy Adams, father of Grantley Adams, the first Premier of

Barbados. He was credited for the expansion of the student roll and creating a school that was disciplined, with high Christian values and a reputation for academic excellence. Succeeding headmasters continued the tradition until the arrival of Charles Wilkinson "Wilkie" Cumberbatch who was appointed headmaster in 1931. Wilkie Cumberbatch was a visionary and clearly mapped out strategies for primary education broadly.

Avis was fortunate to be assigned to St Giles' Boys' School, the premier elementary school on the island under the leadership of Mr Cumberbatch. The erudite headmaster used a system of mentoring to train new teachers. First Avis would spend several weeks observing a senior teacher, acquiring knowledge of teaching, and practising new skills. The proximity of classes also allowed teachers to learn from each other. On the staff of St Giles' Boys' were some of the leading education icons of the day who would later serve at the national level.

Mr Cumberbatch was exceptionally skilled at preparing boys for the Primary to First Grade Scholarship for entry to Harrison College, or the Primary to Second Grade Scholarship to Combermere School. The elect of these students later attended prestigious universities in the United Kingdom; this was the height of accomplishment of a grammar school education. In addition to the academics, Cumberbatch implemented initiatives that were foreign to other schools at the time. Extracurricular activities, with emphasis on athletics, cricket and football were encouraged. Later he would serve as district inspector in the Department of Education. The Wilkie Cumberbatch School bears his name.

Ignatius Byer, son of William Byer also a respected headmaster at St Giles' Boys', was promoted first to headmaster of St Clement's School. He also served as headmaster of West St Joseph School, a secondary school, now Grantley Adams Memorial. Byer was appointed Education Inspector, and later, he was promoted to Senior Education Officer with responsibility for primary schools. The Ignatius Byer Primary School in Lowlands, St Lucy, is named after him.

The Irving Wilson School, is named for its founder and first principal. The noted educator was trained at the Rawle Training Institute at Codrington College and entered the teaching service in 1934. Mr Wilson championed the case for a school for the hearing and visually impaired and was awarded the Barbados Service Star for his pioneering work in Special Education.

Avis established herself as a permanent member of St Giles' Boys' School, despite the odds. Boys were more likely than girls to receive a secondary education and women were unable to compete with them for the limited jobs available in the colony. As a result, male teachers outnumbered female teachers on staff, and taught the older and brighter boys. They earned a higher salary and were more likely to be promoted to higher office. Class assignments were also different. As a female teacher Miss Inniss taught First Primer, the equivalent of the Reception class of five-year-olds, and when streaming was introduced, she was assigned to the B-stream. This skilled teacher who was admired by her students and colleagues, including the headmaster, was never promoted beyond the rank of assistant-teacher.

The staff found Cumberbatch difficult. They laughed at his thick St Lucy accent and described him as "countrified." He was meticulous, and to avoid the headmaster's displeasure, Miss Inniss soon developed an exceptional eye for detail. The boys wore caps, and if one went missing, teachers would be held responsible and receive a reprimand from the headmaster; as she expressed it, "He would take a turn in you." With forty students in the class, this was not an easy task. Using the colour and the size of the hat, the stiffness of the peak, and the height and shape of the crown, she soon devised a strategy to match each boy with his headwear.

Only the highest standards were accepted from teachers and

students alike. Staff members were expected to greet the headmaster with a handshake on arrival and when leaving school, maybe a precursor to clocking in, and females were required to wear stockings. During the daily hygiene checks, boys had to bare their teeth, and fingernails were inspected for cleanliness. Boys were subjected to the pencil test to determine if the hair was combed. Wesley Hall recalled being lashed when the pencil failed to pass through his very curly hair; his brother with straighter hair passed the test easily.

Wes, as he was affectionately called, was one of the students who benefitted from the sports programme initiative. He represented Barbados and the West Indies in cricket and was renowned for his fast bowling. Better known for his prowess on the cricket field, he became a senator, a minister of government, and a minister of the gospel in the Pentecostal Church. He received a knighthood in the Queen's Birthday Honours of 2012 for his contribution to sports and the community.

Wes met Miss Inniss when he was four but had to wait until Class 1, when he was seven to join her class. He remembers her as an outstanding teacher who exhibited the highest standard in dress and speech and was respected in and out of the school. "Miss Inniss exuded love; she was patient, had excellent communication skills, and connected with students easily," he said. He credits his teacher with instilling a sense of confidence in him that led to predictions of what seemed like impossible achievements for that time; passing the exam for admission to Combermere School and qualifying for the West Indies cricket team.

Miss Inniss developed a keen interest in students who fell behind in their academic performance. Absenteeism was a major concern. Children picked "pond grass," a misnomer, as there were several species of weeds which would spread easily and could reduce the yield of food crops. This was done primarily in the vacation, but some children never returned to school; the parents opting instead, to have them earn the ten cents a day to contribute to the limited family income.

Those who were absent returned to school and little, if any, effort was made to provide them with what was taught in their absence. Avis soon became known for the work she did with those students. They sat next to her on the only piece of furniture available—a broken chair with no back—that became known as Miss Inniss' chair. Her colleagues questioned her and could not understand why she bothered with those students who had poor attendance records and were not learning.

The headmaster was a firm disciplinarian and used corporal punishment unsparingly to maintain order and scare the students into performing well. Children were lashed severely for everything: deportment, for being late, for schoolwork and for left-handedness. "Some masters were downright cruel," said a past student when recalling his days at St Giles' Boys'. They revelled in and bragged about their named straps; "sugar daddy," at the end of the arm of a strong, angry teacher was neither fatherly, nor sweet. Then there was "The Grinner" whose face contorted into a menacing grin as he administered the strap. When a tall, tough-looking youngster refused to flinch when being flogged, masters lined up in competition, trying to break his strong will and be the first to make him cry.

In sharp contrast to the "aggressive male beaters on staff," Miss Inniss was remembered fondly by Sir Wes as "firm and serious, but a kind and gentle disciplinarian." She did not think that children should be treated with such cruelty, and this would strongly influence her decision to leave the public service.

Formal teaching training was still in her future, but Miss Inniss had already earned the admiration and respect of her colleagues including the headmaster, Mr Cumberbatch.

The training of teachers in Barbados had its early beginnings in 1847 under the direction of Dr Richard Rawle, a principal at Codrington College in the parish of St John; lectures for teachers were offered when the students studying the priesthood were on vacation. The Rawle

Training Institute was formally established in 1912 at its St John location. As plans were being made for expansion of the institute, an alternative site was found in the Pine, St Michael and in 1948 Erdiston Teachers' Training College was opened at its current location. The college was the premier teacher-training institute in the Caribbean, admitting its first batch of fourteen foreign students in 1954.

The aim of the college:

> to provide a body of specially-trained men and women who are capable of making the most of every child's ability, however great or small, and helping children to become men and women who can give themselves to the community in which they live rather than being a charge upon it.

Avis Carrington would be a wife and mother before registering for training at the college. Her qualifications, the Junior and Senior Cambridge certificates and fourteen years' teaching experience far exceeded the requirements: one school certificate and at least five years' experience for matriculation at the teachers' college.

The course of study included English, mathematics, social studies, religious knowledge, health, physical education, music, home economics, woodwork, gardening, visual aids, and art. In addition, the student teachers completed principles of education and school management. Another important aspect of the programme was the invitation of specialists from a variety of fields who shared their vast knowledge and skills with the students.

In the practical component, teachers were observed and supervised by the permanent staff of the college at Erdiston Model School, which was established for that purpose. Additional schools were used when the number of students increased. The Model School eventually became Erdiston Primary School and continued at this location until its merger in 2009 with Carrington Primary School situated in Carrington's Village. The resulting George Lamming Primary School on Bridge Road in St Michael was named for Barbados' most distinguished novelist.

During this period, Erdiston was led by A. W. Roberts, a former Assistant Director of Education. He was assisted by vice principal Jack Bentley and eight tutors. The principal lived in a private residence on campus, and the vice principal's quarters were upstairs of the main building where classes were taught. The college was residential, with separate dorms for male and female students. These were shared and roommates were rotated at the end of every term to allow for full integration. The students shared common academic interests, exchanged ideas, practised their skills, and participated in social activities while building a sense of community. Avis and her peers developed long-lasting personal and professional relationships. She spoke fondly of her roommate, the late Muriel Norgrove, who taught at Foundation Girls' School and her daughter Jasmine who was a student at Merrivale.

Complaints of the noise level coming from downstairs of the Bentley family residence were frequent, as students participated in lively class discussion. Avis was the vice president of the student body and her colleague, Mattison Hall, was president. Their roles were not clearly defined, but they were sometimes invited to tea, and revelled in the privilege of joining the principal at his residence. Avis thought that there could have been more student participation in class but never raised the issue. But the case of the unidentified floaters in the split pea soup came up for discussion with her peers.

Erdiston was only two years old at the time, when this minor issue was brought to the attention of the student government; black specks had been spotted floating in the split-pea soup. No sign of an infestation was seen when the peas were purchased; the weevil eggs were hidden deep inside the seeds but later hatched into larvae, which grew into the black mature adults. The housekeeper was distraught and apologised profusely. Instead of protest, the situation generated much laughter, and the student reps settled back into an uneventful term of service.

Today, Erdiston Teachers' Training College offers programmes in collaboration with the University of the West Indies. These include training for teachers, management training for school administrators, and since September of 2016 a Bachelor of Education programme. In addition, the Division of Continuing Education offers a range of evening classes to educators and members of the public. Currently, about ninety-four per cent of full-time teachers in the public system are trained and certified, and return for ongoing training.

After completion of the one-year programme, Avis Carrington was awarded the Teacher's Certificate and returned to St Giles' Boys' grounded in education theory and equipped with new teaching strategies. Instead of an emphasis on having students solve hard sums, she now had a broader perspective on teaching and learning. The educator who influenced her most was Dr Maria Montessori, whose methods revolutionised teaching worldwide. The medical doctor, turned educator, demonstrated that children with learning difficulties could acquire skills never before imagined, and could score above average on state tests. Avis Carrington shared with Montessori the need for individualised instruction, hands-on, child-friendly methods, and a happy and stress-free environment. Her views contrasted significantly with the school climate at St Giles' Boys'; but another eight years would pass before she could create an alternative teaching and learning environment for children, one that was in keeping with her philosophy of education.

FIVE

"You don't choose your family. They are God's gift to you, as you are to them." —Desmond Tutu

Vere and Avis on their wedding day.
Avis' Uncle Ghent is standing in on his late brother's behalf.

The Carringtons

AVIS Inniss felt ready to start a family, but there was one major concern: Where would she find a suitor who would earn her father's respect and, furthermore, be brave enough to ask for her hand in marriage? This question was answered when Erdine met two brothers while visiting her relatives in St Andrew. Back at the family home, she shared the story of the chance meeting of the two young men who impressed her with their good looks, fine manners and charm. Erdine was twenty-two years old, and it was very likely that Arthur Byer had already shown an interest; but she made sure to mention her two younger sisters.

Between giggles and the occasional tease, Erdine would not stop talking about the two young men, but neither of the girls seemed eager to meet her friends. Her sisters thought it futile to show any interest. They knew their father's demeanour; he was not yet ready to allow young men near his home or for his daughters to start courting. Dan was always one to please her father and would comply, and up until that time, Avis had shown no interest in boys, apart from a secret crush she had on one of her colleagues. At age eighteen she was still having fun planning exploits with her sister Erdine, but all this would change when Avis met Vere.

Vere Carrington was the last of three sons born to Barbadian parents in Trinidad and Tobago. His father, Lawrence Newton Carrington, and mother, Evangeline Carrington, were devout Moravians, one of the denominations that had brought Christianity and education to the enslaved population in the region. Lawrence, followed in his father's footsteps and was a teacher in Barbados; he adopted the twin-island colony as his home when he was transferred to teach at Gloster Lodge Moravian School opened in 1895 in Port of Spain. Lawrence Carrington was a quiet person of a reserved nature, but a zealous teacher as described by his peers; and he was well loved by his students.

By the time Vere was born in 1915, his father had already risen to prominence. In 1902 he arrived from Barbados with a 4th Class Teacher's Certificate. Later, he completed the Class 1 certificate and was promoted to headmaster. He made a name for himself and was well respected by the authorities. He was also an ardent member of the Elementary Teachers' Union, and was known for his sound advice. A valued member of the Moravian Church, he rose to the level of superintendent of the Sunday School. His last public appearance was on Monday 1st August 1921, where he presented a farewell speech on behalf of the Moravian Community. Reverend Theodor Clemens was the Superintendent of the Moravian Mission in Trinidad. He had completed his mission, and was returning to the United Kingdom.

Sadly a few weeks later, Lawrence died suddenly. Having lost the bread winner of the family, the younger boys, six-year-old Vere and his eight-year-old brother Deighton returned to Barbados with their mother.

Fearing the interruption of Harold's education, he was left in Trinidad with friends of the family. He excelled at school and was the recipient of a college exhibition from Gloster Lodge Moravian School.

Harold and his wife settled in Trinidad and raised three children: Vicky, Lawrence, who was given his grandfather's name, and Trevor.

Vere was six feet tall and strikingly handsome, but Avis showed little interest at first; their friendship would develop over time. She grew to admire his calm, reserved and composed nature, traits he inherited from his father. As a young adult, Vere had already identified his goals and ambitions for the future, and she was particularly impressed with his desire to serve in the Royal Air Force (RAF) of the United Kingdom.

Vere was an outstanding student. He excelled at elementary school and won a Primary to First Grade Scholarship to Harrison College, one of the premier secondary schools for boys in the region. He completed the curriculum which included classical and mathematical studies in preparation for the Barbados Scholarship, which ensured admission to the Universities of Oxford and Cambridge.

This scholarship, which was solely intended for boys, was introduced as part of the recommendations of the Mitchinson Commission of 1875. It would not be made available to girls until 1903. An inadequate programme, no better than that of the second-grade school for boys, prevented girls from competing on equal terms with their male counterparts. As a result, the award was not granted to a female until 1946, when Elsie Pilgrim (later Payne) became the first girl to receive the prized Barbados Scholarship. Dame Elsie Payne became the first native headmistress of Queen's College and was the first woman in Barbados to receive the award, Dame of St Andrew, for her contribution to education.

A case of Bell's palsy, a paralysis of the facial nerve, caused Vere to miss valuable school time and he failed to reach the requirements for the Barbados Scholarship. However, he was awarded the less prestigious Island Scholarship in 1935 and a place at Codrington College. Established in 1745, the seminary prepared students in the disciplines of philosophy and divinity. In 1875, it was affiliated to Durham

University in the United Kingdom and offered a tertiary programme. The University of the West Indies (UWI) has been conducting the theology programmes of the Faculty of the Humanities and Education at the St John institution since 1965. Vere started preparation for the priesthood, but after one year he suspended his studies. He had already identified an alternative career path and a course of study, but the chance meeting with Erdine would postpone his plans and alter his destiny.

Vere and his brother Deighton sought employment in the Civil Service, but the commute from St Andrew to Bridgetown was a difficult undertaking. The Barbados Railway ceased operation in 1937, and the only remaining transportation options were horse and buggy or "M2," a playful reference to travelling by foot. The pair decided to settle in the city at the home of their great aunt, where Vere spent weekdays during school time; on weekends, he made the long walk back to his home in St Andrew.

Eventually, the young men moved to a rental property in Government Hill, a short distance from the Inniss home. Thoughts of meeting Erdine never left their minds, and they were both eager to meet her sisters. Soon after taking up residence in the area, Vere and Deighton kept a promise they had made to visit the Inniss home. The girls had grown into fine young ladies, graceful and elegant in their speech and dress, and each had a pleasant demeanour, but at five feet four inches, and nineteen years old at the time, the petite and charming Avis, with the demure smile, was the one who caught Vere's eye.

A visit to see Mr Inniss' daughters was a visit to see the whole family. He would pull up a chair and engage Vere and Deighton in discussions about the issues of the day, enquire about their family, and question them on their plans for the future. This was simply a ploy to determine their suitability as future sons-in-law, and to make sure that these young men were not left alone with his daughters. As they sat with Papa,

Erdine and Avis were already hatching a plan to circumvent their over-protective father.

The plot unfolded in two parts. Papa was reluctant, but the girls were old enough to attend the Exhibition on their own. Their older cousin Arthur Byer would be in attendance, and that gave him some comfort. Despite their father's vigilance, the girls managed to communicate their intention to meet the Carrington boys in Queen's Park. Part two called for the skills of the chief prankster. The long-established curfew was four o'clock, but before leaving home, Erdine turned the hands of the clock back by an hour to allow more time for the rendezvous.

The young ladies "stole the show" in their fashionable dresses, and the young men were equally impressive in their dapper suits and felt hats. The group of six settled into a pleasant afternoon; Arthur accompanied Erdine and Vere escorted Avis. Deighton was present, but Dan insisted that she was in the company of everyone. Unaware that prying eyes were everywhere, they took full advantage of the "extra hour." But these were the old-time days, and the village, however one viewed it, took its role of raising a child seriously. Before they arrived back home, wagging tongues had told the tale and soon, they would answer to Papa for their youthful indiscretion.

Avis and Erdine were allies who had challenged the status quo repeatedly. On the other hand, Dan was the one who always conformed to her parents' expectations, and in return she earned special sway with their father. Now they were in trouble and dependent on her for a favourable outcome. But would she come to their rescue?

The interrogation was intense and intimidating and made that much worse because they had all let Papa down. The group was relieved when Dan described the outing as "a mere gathering of friends," knowing as she did that Erdine was paired with Arthur, they would later marry; and Vere had fallen for Avis, and she was equally smitten.

When Avis met Vere, they were both employed. This fitted well with their plans to start a family. She had started her career in the teaching service, and he was a public servant. Avis' salary of twelve dollars per month was given to her mother who managed her finances; she was granted a small allowance when needed, and the balance was deposited in her savings account. Avis' prospects for furthering her education and future chances of promotion were limited. However, Vere would become a public servant and be promoted to the highest administrative level in the public service.

One other issue, the marriage bar could have influenced Avis' decision to choose between her teaching career and starting a family. This was the mandatory termination of employment of married women from the Public Service, especially after they became mothers. Beatrice Inniss, Avis' mother was forced to forfeit her nursing career when she became a wife and mother. Even so, Miss Inniss had reason to be optimistic. Mrs Lewis, the headmistress at Belmont Girls' School was married and a mother of four. In the early Forties, the Barbados Elementary Schools' Teacher Association, the precursor of the Barbados Union of Teachers, had fought and won the right for married female teachers to remain in the system, and to be reinstated after pregnancy and childbirth.

*

The facts are sketchy, but it seems as if there was brief competition on either side. Vere had a secret admirer; however, by the time her interest was made known, he had already fallen for Avis. And Avis had a crush on a dashing colleague before she met Vere. He was admired by the females on staff at St Giles' Boys', not only for his good looks but he was one that Avis could emulate as she observed teachers practising their craft.

But it was Miss Inniss who earned herself bragging rights. The school was a few yards from her home and she walked to and from work every day; but now she was regretting its proximity. After falling ill at work, her secret crush offered to drive her home. She climbed into the car all starry-eyed, and her discomfort soon disappeared. But before her racing heart could settle down and allow her to soak in the pleasure of his company, the short ride had come to an end.

At eleven-years old Wes Hall was way too young to be a suitor, but at a speech to mark the 30th anniversary of Merrivale, he made clear the feelings he had for his teacher and the heartache he felt on learning that Vere had won her hand.

Papa died before Vere proposed to Avis. "There was mention of prostate trouble, no one talked about cancer back then," Avis explained. This left Mama to supervise the budding romance. She eased the rules, allowing the couple time to get to know each other, until Vere wrote to his future mother-in-law asking for Avis' hand in marriage. The ceremony was held on 6 December, 1947 at St Matthias Church in Christ Church. He was thirty-one and she was twenty-nine. The bride wore a traditional white sheath dress, accessorised with a white pearl necklace and stud earrings. A two-tiered cathedral-length veil followed the radiant bride down the aisle. The bouquet of loosely arranged flowers, purchased from the Self Help on upper Broad Street in the city, was a gift from her mother's friends. The groom wore a classic suit with a minimal single-flower boutonnière.

Family and friends gathered at the family home in the Ivy for a grand reception. The villagers turned out in their numbers and seized every vantage point to get a glimpse of the radiant bride as she posed for pictures on the arm of her husband. In the background was Henry, called Uncle Ghent, by his nieces. He stood as the father-giver during the ceremony and was now monitoring the proceedings on his late brother's behalf.

The newlyweds rented properties close to Avis' childhood home in the Ivy, increasing the distance each time they changed residence, yet never moving far away. The first home was in Two Mile Hill; they then lived in Government Hill before moving to Welches, where the noted educator Louis Lynch was a neighbour. Avis would become Godmother to their daughter Jan, and Marjorie, Louis' wife godmother to Avis' son Ian. In 1956, the family moved into their own home, "Shenstone," at Number 15, Pine Road, on the eastern end of Belleville. The district is made up of eleven parallel avenues that run east to west; George Street borders the western end of the enclave.

Established in the late eighteenth century, this private residential area was developed by Sam Manning, founder of DaCosta Manning, and his business partner George Whitfield. It was one of the first suburbs in Barbados with a distinctive architectural style. The houses were a mix of Caribbean Georgian with parapet roofs, open and enclosed jalousie porches, hooded sash windows, and ornate lattice and fret work.

The landscaping was iconic. In 1885, nine-hundred royal palms (Roystonea) were planted in rows that lined both sides of each avenue. The ringed cylindrical trunks of these majestic palms shoot straight into the sky and explode into suspended bunches of fan leaves. Uncharacteristic for the area was a residential community with its smaller wooden houses located between what is today the Sagicor Complex on 1st Avenue Belleville and Pine Road. At the north-western corner of Pine Road and Collymore Rock was "Miss Walcott Shop," a grocery store that served the area for several years.

Belleville was also known for its racial segregation. Up until 1935 public access to the first seven avenues was restricted. Black men were not allowed in the area after six o'clock, but black women who were employed as maids were tolerated. Vere was not deterred by the prejudice. There was no law preventing him from owning property in Belleville and the young barrister, now called an attorney at law or lawyer, and his wife Avis, a respected teacher, purchased a home in the development.

Two other black families who were friends of the Carringtons lived in Belleville; none lived on Pine Road. The Piles, Kenneth and his mother

Erica, lived on the Third Avenue and the Harrisons, Lisle and Marjorie and their three sons lived on the Fourth Avenue. They were both considered "high brown"; in the local dialect meaning light-coloured skin with straight to wavy hair.

Racial prejudice was evident in St Cyprian Church, at the corner of 7th Avenue Belleville and George Street, where the Carringtons worshipped. The whites, who were considered the upper class, sat at the front of the sanctuary in reserved pews. Vere had no "airs and graces" about himself and even though he was a resident of the area, the family first sat at the back of the church. By the time Ian, the Carrington's youngest son, was old enough to remember, the family was sitting in the middle of the church. The villagers sat at the very back. This practice continued long after segregation in the church was discontinued, as if they "knew their place."

"Shenstone," the Carringtons' home, was situated opposite 4th Avenue, Belleville. The large front yard was reduced by a third when the government acquired land to build a pedestrian footpath. A double flight of opposing stairs with elegant wrought-iron railings merged at the entrance to a sprawling L-shaped veranda that ran north halfway across the front of the house before making a right angle turn to the east. Two wooden doors with glazed glass panels opened on either side of the coral-stone bungalow and led to a spacious living room. The other rooms were fitted with large hooded sash windows that completed the period home. The three-bedroom, one-bathroom house was later renovated to include an additional bathroom. When Vere returned from his studies in England, he found that the space beneath the dining room had been excavated to build him a study.

Vere and Avis had three children—two boys and one girl—all born before the move to Pine Road. The first son was born in 1948. Avis wanted to name him after his father Vere, whose second name was Ian. "But he just did not look like an Ian," Avis explained. She chose the name Ronald instead, because of a very well-behaved student in her class with that name. Like his mum, Ronnie preferred an alternative version of his name. Three years later, Shelley seemed eager to join the family and arrived days before the due date. When it became clear that the expectant mother would not make it to the hospital on time, a midwife was called to assist with the delivery. When she arrived at the home, she was greeted by the cries of the newest member of the Carrington family. In 1955, Avis gave birth to her third child, a son, and this time, he looked like an "Ian."

Vere, called Dad by the children, was a loving and supportive husband and father who provided a comfortable space for his children to flourish and for Avis to pursue her passion. He was measured and conservative, of impeccable character and an excellent role model. Avis admired his patience with their children and how he involved himself in every aspect of their lives. Vere assisted with homework and was never too busy to listen to stories or answer questions. And seemingly out of character, he enjoyed time spent horsing around with the children.

Vere's caring nature extended beyond the home. As an attorney at law, he was a mentor to young persons in his field and provided legal advice free of cost to clients who could not afford to pay. He sometimes made loans available to those in need and negotiated repayment plans that were best suited to the debtor.

Avis, called Mum by the children, was a warm and nurturing mother; Ronnie her eldest son found her, "firm but fair," "a very balanced mother." She showed her love through her deeds, but ever the teacher, her enthusiasm and demand for academic excellence went farther than most parents. Schoolwork was kept under close surveillance and she subjected the children to frequent coaching sessions; always reminding them to emulate their father, who was, "very bright," and that he "missed out on the Barbados Scholarship only because of illness."

This intensity was balanced with a range of social activities; birthday parties, fairs, theatre, cinema, an evening at a visiting circus with clowns, acrobats and daring animal acts with lions and tigers; or Coney Island, a travelling amusement company with breath-taking rides, a roller coaster and sideshows. In 1967, Mum and the children, travelled to Canada and the United States of America, a trip that was deliberately rich with educational activities: Expo 67, Niagara Falls, Times Square, a ferry ride around Manhattan, and shows at Madison Square Garden and Radio City Music Hall.

Mum always prepared breakfast and supper; the Sunday evening special was ham sandwiches with a touch of Neville Edwards hot sauce, a local brand which continued to be favoured by the family. She feigned indifference when asked, but the requested items would always be found under the Christmas tree. Her support for the children's academic success was demonstrated when she took the time, after long, tiring days of teaching and running the school, to take a refresher course in French to assist Shelley who was struggling with the language.

Dad did not shy away from disciplining the children, but it was Mum who was strict and the chief enforcer of rules. She perfected "the look" and used the threat of "the strap," which was regarded with trepidation; these were often enough to ensure good behaviour. In contrast, she could smother the children with a reassuring embrace when needed; or soothe a persistent cough by lovingly applying Vicks and Buckley's to a congested chest to ensure a good night's rest.

As manager of housekeeping, Mum made sure each child participated in chores, including the periodic purging of "Shenstone." Packaging, including empty cardboard boxes and wrapping paper, books deemed to be obsolete, and anything that had outlived its usefulness were added to piles that grew on the floor of each room before they were lugged to their final destination on "the hill." The boys, cutlass in hand, cleared a path through the dense foliage to the burning pit at the most eastern edge of the property. Fuelled with kerosene, the trash became a roaring monster of red and yellow flames that consumed everything in range before calming to a flicker. As a precaution, the garden hose was dragged, reluctantly it always seemed, to put out every last ember.

Avis cherished the close relationship with her mother and it continued into her marriage. Gran lived at the Back Ivy residence but spent two days each week at Pine Road, where she helped with the children and assisted with cooking. This continued until her death in 1978, at the age of ninety-four. Aunt Dan had no children of her own and lived at the family home with her mother until her move to the headmistress' residence at St Michael's Girls' School in 1963. She took on the role of second mother to her nieces and nephew.

Arthur Byer was already a member of the family and a frequent visitor to his uncle Robert's home. His marriage to Erdine, who was adopted by the Innisses, was the origin of the Byer branch of the family. They eloped in 1940, but their living arrangements fell through, and Papa made it clear that the young couple could not live together in his home. Arthur continued to live with his family in St George, leaving his wife at her childhood home. On the rare occasion that Arthur slept over, and only on account of bad weather, he and his wife were not allowed to share a bedroom.

Arthur and Erdine eventually moved to St George, first to Sweet Bottom, where they spent about twelve years before settling into what was the master's house on a small plantation in Harmony Cottage in the same parish. The couple presented the Inniss family with their first grandchild, Pat, who was born in 1942. The family doubled when the couple added three other daughters—Hazel, Cheryl and Averil. A-A as Avis is called by her nieces, is great aunt to Erdine's six grandchildren— Ryan, Sherral (who is called Cherrie), Keisha, Rasheda, Renaldo, and Christopher.

The affection shared between Avis and her siblings as young girls continued into their adulthood. The bond between Avis and Erdine grew even stronger after the birth of their children. The arrivals of the Carrington and Byer children were staggered; this was not planned of course, but it allowed the families to share a single crib and christening gown with matching bonnet designed by Erdine. The interchangeable lace ribbon was pink or blue depending on the sex of the child. Just like Mama Inniss, Erdine became Godma to all of the children when she became Shelley's godmother in 1951.

*

Avis and her sisters loved gardening, a hobby they inherited from their mother. The acre of land at Harmony Cottage grew an orchard of fruit trees with colourful shrubs and an abundance of vegetable and flower gardens. Many plant cuttings made their way to Martindale's Road and Pine Road where the sisters lived; St Michael's Girls and Merrivale students attended schools with well-tended gardens that featured an array of flowers and rich foliage.

The cousins also developed their own special relationships: Ronnie and Hazel, Pat and Shelley, and the younger cousins Cheryl, Averil and Ian. Summer vacations were split between the two homes, half of the time at Pine Road and the other half at Harmony Cottage, allowing the parents a much-needed break. The Byer girls adored their aunt A-A. She was always pleasant, patient and nurturing. The Carrington children enjoyed their romps in the country. They loved Godma's calm and easy spirit, but most of all they looked forward to her cooking and baking, especially her coconut bread.

By 1959, Avis was eleven years into her marriage and had settled into a life of comfort and ease. She had supported Vere in his quest to further his education and was satisfied that he had completed the correspondent component of the law degree. After he was called to the Bar at Gray's Inn in London, he returned to Barbados to practise law; but first he would continue his public service and be promoted to Permanent Secretary in the Ministry of Labour.

The joint incomes of Vere and Avis afforded them a lifestyle that included family outings to "bay houses," properties close to the beach that were rented as guest houses in Bathsheba in St Joseph and Martin's Bay in St John. Avis was an Erdiston-trained teacher and had settled into her chosen career, but after two decades in the public service she had not seen the changes in primary schooling that she anticipated, and she had no power to implement or even influence a change to a child-centred approach to teaching. This left a void that needed to be filled. The decision would not be easy, but after a period of reflection, Avis felt certain in her judgment. It was time for an addition to the family.

'Shenstone'

No. 15 Pine Road. The family home from 1957, and Merrivale Preparatory School from 1959 until 2010.

Family in all its forms.

Above: The Maxwells with baby Melvin who was
adopted by the Carringtons after his parents passed away, and
the Carrington siblings, from left: Ronnie, Ian and Shelley.

Opposite, top: The Carringtons circa 1975. From left, Ronnie,
Shelley, Avis, Vere, Beatrice Inniss (Gran) and Ian.

Opposite: Avis with Shelley, Ian (centre) and Ronnie.

Above: Avis and Vere on their 25th wedding anniversary, 1972; and, left, in 1978.

Opposite: The family gathering was held at the Byers, Christmas 1985. Constance is seated first from right and Erdine third from right in the second row. Avis is standing in front of Vere, back left. The Byer siblings are Pat, second from left, Hazel, first from left in the second row and Cheryl is fourth from right. This was Uncle Arthur's (seated in red shirt) last Christmas.

Sharing a love of plants, Avis and daughter-in-law Hazel, at the Flower and Garden Show at Balls Plantation with grandchildren Julian and Ria.

Below: In 2001, Avis spent Christmas in Vienna; seen here with granddaughters Kori, left, and Ria.

Avis, left, visits her sister Dan who is celebrating her 99th birthday.

SIX

"One test of the correctness of educational procedure is the happiness of the child." —Maria Montessori

The playgroup that mushroomed into Merrivale Preparatory School, first met in the spacious dining room at 'Shenstone.' (Photo courtesy Toni Jones, Terra.)

Something Attempted

EVERY weekday morning, Avis walked the distance from Pine Road to St Giles' Boys' School in the Ivy. Her husband Vere Carrington, the magistrate for the Eastern District in St Philip, left home early and drove the older children to school. Eleven-year-old Ronnie was in first form at Harrison College, and Shelley, who was seven, attended St Gabriel's School. Ian, three, was a happy child who spent carefree days being pampered by Gran and Smith, his babysitter.

That was until a marked change in his behaviour. Ian had grown tired of his morning routine, it seemed, and longed to attend school like his older siblings. Ian would chime in with made up stories when Ronnie and Shelley were asked about their day at school. And each morning he became increasingly agitated when he was left behind. A ride from the garage to the front gate had been successful in calming him, but on a morning that would change the trajectory of Avis' life, the child was inconsolable.

The babysitter lifted Ian from the car with a caring and joyful spirit, but this could not slow the trickle that had started in the corner of his eyes. Gran tried to soothe him, but this only served to elevate the theatrics. His tepid whimper soon changed into cries of despair, and he unleashed a flood of tears that flowed freely down his cheeks. Avis made one last attempt to calm him before she left for work.

"Smith loves you," she tried to assure him in a gentle tone. "She will take good care of you."

"No, Mum," he pleaded, between sniffles and a doleful sigh. "Smith just wouldn't do!"

The uneasiness Avis felt when leaving her son at home soon grew into feelings of guilt. Every day as she walked the mile-long distance to work north along Pine Road, east on Government Hill before turning left on to Ivy Road she carried this burden of uncertainty; and with every step she took, Avis pondered her next move. She could no longer ignore the needs of her three-year-old son. He certainly could not be left at home for another two years before attending elementary school at age five. A change had to come.

Mr Cumberbatch's insistence that female staff wear stockings to school was not a major factor when making her decision, but it may have had some influence. Irving Wilson recalled a determined Miss Inniss, bolstered by the backing of her colleagues, arguing that the accessory had become scarce after the Second World War, which lasted from 1939 until 1945. The headmaster relented, and the ladies won the right to bare what little leg was exposed in those days. But other, more pressing issues were up for deliberation.

After twenty-three years in the public service, Avis Carrington pondered the likelihood of becoming a headteacher, or an inspector of schools. For the most part, these positions were reserved for males; only one female colleague from St Giles' Boys', Iris Riley had become a headmistress. Avis was not prepared to chance her destiny on an uncer-tain future policy that might increase her prospects for promotion. She was aware how slow change was in colonial Barbados.

The marriage bar had been rescinded in the early forties, but wage disparity based on the sex of the employee was not rectified until 1965, twenty-nine years after her teaching career started. Another ten years would pass before the declaration of the United Nations Decade of Women (1976-1985), and the formation of the Commission on the Status of Women in 1978, to identify and redress gender imbalances in Barbados.

Avis had the benefit of teaching at a highly rated school, but the memories of her elementary school continued to haunt her daily and she grew increasingly concerned about her inability to bring change to the current school setting. She described the school culture as rigid; children were to be seen and not heard and could not dare question a teacher's opinion. They had to respond in a particular way and were not allowed to express themselves freely. And the punishment of children was cruel and excessive.

Some saw Avis Carrington as a visionary and a risk-taker, but she saw herself as neither. She was influenced by the Montessori methods and was ready to demonstrate that children could be happy while learning. But the real reason for the shift from public service to starting her own private school was her motherly instincts. She was merely responding to the needs of her three-year-old son whose protest was becoming more intense every day.

After observing a small private school in the Ivy that was run by a lone female, she felt that she could do the same. The only thing left was to discuss the idea with her family. Vere listened with patience and was supportive. Her mother encouraged her and was a ready source of help. Erdine believed in her sister's ability and did not question her judgment, but Dan was apprehensive. She thought that Avis could easily become a headmistress in the public teaching service. Ronnie was twelve years old at the time and showed little interest. Two years later he moved in with aunt Dan at the St Michael's Girls' School residence, leaving his siblings to discover the implications of this new venture.

Shelley was excited at the thought of having new playmates. As for Ian, not only would he have his mother at home, but his new friends would come over to play every day. If Ray, the family pet, could have seen into the future, he would have been the only dissenter. The golden retriever was nervous around children and had to be locked away when school was in session.

Avis' colleagues were ambivalent about her move. They were sad to see her go because they treasured her outstanding service. A few warned of the risk of leaving a secure government job for the uncertainty of private enterprise. But they rallied around her, knowing that among the qualities they admired was her determination. Armed with this vote of confidence, Avis Carrington walked away from a permanent post at St Giles' Boys' School and the possibility, however slim, of a promotion later in her career. Her earnings had grown from twelve dollars per month in 1936 to one hundred dollars by the time she resigned. She was sure of the location, and had already thought of a name for the playgroup; but one last challenge remained. Where was she to find the children?

Avis Carrington had first-hand knowledge from her childhood of how fear could negatively impact academic progress. As a result, she was confident in her effort and committed to the task of creating a space where children could learn at their own pace and, most importantly, where they would be happy.

Her synonym of choice was "merry." By applying the rule that changes "y" to "i" when adding a suffix, "Merrivale" was created. "Preparatory" was added when the role of the school evolved from playgroup to the preparation of students for the Barbados Secondary Schools' Entrance Examination (common entrance, also called the 11-plus). However, for all its years, Merrivale Preparatory School was still better known as "Miss Carrington School."

The founding of the school was timely. Upper-class families were

already taking advantage of the well-established private primary schools of the day to increase their chances of gaining entry to a
grammar school: Codrington School, St Angela's Junior, the primary
level of St Ursula's, which was also called The Ursuline Convent School;
St Gabriel's School and St Winifred's School. Merrivale Preparatory
School provided an alternative for the emerging black middle class,
with fees that were more affordable.

*

The coral-stone bungalow at Number 15, Pine Road, sat on twenty-four
thousand square feet of land, nestled between a row of giant mahogany
trees at the front and a variety of other species which stood guard on the
gentle rise towards the eastern end of the property. The dense canopy
provided cover for an undergrowth of colourful shrubs: a white frangi-
pani; the pinks, reds and purples of bougainvillea; a variety of crotons
with fiery red and mottled green leaves accented with bright yellow
veins; these stood out against a backdrop of evergreen palm trees, each
with its characteristic fronds and textured trunks.

Four distinct areas made up the garden. When the family moved
in, the elevated area to the east of the house was covered with dense,
mangled bushes and was only accessible through an opening in the
fence. In his early teens, Ronnie wielded a cutlass like a man and was
eager to take on the task of levelling the overgrowth. He cleared the hill
of the bush, and over time Avis transformed the landscape. A stack of
concrete steps lead up to this raised area which is separated from the
main garden, by a retaining wall.

Two lawns laid out like soft green carpets sat on either side of a tiled
area, the clay weathered to a rustic charm. A large mango tree domi-
nated this space, and in its shadow, concentric rings of potted plants
created a display of shapes, textures and hues at the base of the tree. The
bold, speckled dieffenbachia leaves contrasted with the delicate fronds

of various species of ferns, and anthuriums and coleus (Joseph's coat) added a pop of colour. Separating the western lawn was a greenhouse covered with bright yellow allamanda that charmingly lost its way while providing shade for plants that preferred filtered light. Hedges manicured to perfection framed the lawns on the outer side, and on the inner, a rainbow of flowering herbs dotted the beds of rich brown soil. For the Carringtons, this was home, but on 15 September 1959, three lucky children were the first of hundreds to call it school.

One of the first students was St Elmo Wilson, the son of a former colleague and mentor, Irving Wilson. He was the first of many educators who sought out Avis Carrington to teach their children. After stints at Ebenezer, Shrewsbury and St Luke's, Wilson joined the staff at St Giles' Boys' School in 1943 where he met the young Avis Inniss. He admired his colleague immensely and described her as his "favourite teacher." Mr Wilson was immediately taken with her outstanding work and was happy to see the progress she had made.

After working with Avis for sixteen years, Mr Wilson had absolutely no hesitation in enrolling his five-year-old son at Merrivale. "I don't think there was a better female teacher in the island," he said. "She was brilliant." He had seen in her many of the qualities of the great Wilkie Cumberbatch: a dedication to teaching in general, her attention to detail, ensuring that pupils strived for perfection in their writing, and a commitment to excellence. But he was particularly impressed with her interest in and dedication to those students who needed additional support.

Avis assembled her small playgroup in the dining room, where sunlight and cooling breezes streamed through the large sash windows. A polished mahogany table with six cane-bottom chairs sat in the centre of the room, and a Berbice Chair—an armchair with long arms and built-in leg rests, occupied one of two corners of the open room. This was the sole classroom in the early days. The living room with its upholstered sectional suite, accent tables and hanging artwork was out of bounds, cordoned off with the single blackboard.

The area was a mix of small, wooden, rectangular tables painted in yellow, each could sit four children in their tiny rush bottom chairs. They were keen and eager to engage with the abundance of teaching resources: alphabet blocks, counters, shapes, puzzles, flashcards, toys and books. Avis varied the teaching methods that included singing, movement, the manipulation of objects and play, all to ensure that the children had fun while learning.

The writing surface was a rectangular piece of slate, a dark grey rock, framed with wood; pencils were made of a softer, lighter coloured slate which was erasable. These writing tools were later replaced with more current paper exercise books and wooden pencils with a core of graphite. The fountain pen and later the ballpoint pen were used by older children and were not allowed at primary schools.

Avis' dream of starting a small playgroup where children could have fun while learning was realised, and close friends of the family soon enrolled their pre-school children. The brother and sister pair of Jeffrey and Margaret Craig, children of the late politician Lionel (Lammy) Craig, and St Elmo Wilson joined Ian for a total of four students on opening day. Two weeks later, cousins Patricia Morris and Gerry Phillips were registered. Hallam Hope enrolled in October, increasing the roll to seven. By the end of the first year, the school population had grown to twelve.

Word soon spread of the new private school, and the numbers increased rapidly, doubling by the end of the second year. The roll would eventually exceed two hundred.

A primary school was not part of her original plan, but the children were fast approaching eleven and time for transfer to secondary school. As a result, the role of the school gradually evolved from that of playgroup to the preparation of students for the common entrance examination. The school cemented its identity when uniforms were introduced in 1962.

"Linda Clarke wore to school the cutest little dress that took my fancy," Avis said.

Using this as her inspiration, her sister Erdine designed the first sample. The sleeveless royal blue tunic with two oversized patch pockets was fastened down the front with four conspicuous white buttons; this was worn by the infant girls, ages four to seven. For the older girls, eight to eleven, the upper part of the garment was a short sleeve blouse with six white buttons arranged in horizontal rows of two, which gave the appearance of a double-breasted style; the skirt was box pleated. Both garments featured the signature sailor collar that first captured Avis' eye. White bias binding arranged in rows of three was used to accentuate the collars, pockets and sleeves, and ran horizontally around the whole width of the skirt. The boys wore khaki short pants and shirts, as was the custom at most primary schools of the time; both boys and girls wore laced black or brown shoes with matching socks to complete what would become a distinct Merrivale look.

*

The school gradually joined the ranks of the established private primary schools. These existed alongside public schools throughout the development of education in Barbados but were unregulated until 1945, when guidelines were laid down by the Department of Education, later the Ministry of Education. Any place where more than ten children were normally gathered for the purpose of instruction had to be registered. Information regarding the premises, type of instruction, and the qualifications of the staff were required. Failing to adhere to these guidelines could result in the withdrawal of permission to operate the school.

Some schools were first established and later sanctioned for operation by the Department of Education. Leacock's Private School in Speightstown, St Peter, was founded in 1948 and operated for two years before an education officer observed the facilities and approved its registration. Vere, Avis' husband, did not hesitate to send a letter to the Ministry of Education with information of the opening of Merrivale. He was a senior civil servant, and even though none was expected, he knew that the authorities should be notified. The school received an informal go-ahead from then Minister of Education, Cameron Tudor. As of August 1990, a private school or education institution cannot be established without the prior approval of the Minister of Education. The Chief Education Officer certifies a copy of approved private schools annually, and these are published in *The Official Gazette.*

As word of "Miss Carrington School" on Pine Road spread, the school's population increased rapidly. One class soon became two, and the single blackboard was used as the only partition. But the school soon outgrew the indoor space and spilled on to the veranda. Leaving the younger students behind in the dining room and moving to the class on the outside soon became a "rite of passage" for the older students. They saw themselves as seniors with elevated rank, albeit self-conferred. This status came with the benefit of a cooler, outdoor "classroom" with nature's built-in teaching resources: the colours and shapes of the flora and fauna; a curious whistling frog that stayed up too late; the force of gravity on a falling mango; the scent of flowers; the music of chirping birds in flight; the spectrum of a suspended rainbow.

The school was only in its sixth year when it became apparent that additional room had to be found. Vere retired from the government service early and used his gratuity to fund the project. He stayed behind while the family vacationed in the United States in the summer of 1967 to oversee the construction of the school building. Burnup and Sims, an American-based construction company, undertook the task of excavating the site and flattening the bottom of the incline to the east of the house to create the foundation. Leslie Murray, the contractor, managed the extension project and built the structure. Friendly and reliable, he established a lifelong business relationship with the family and maintained the home and the school buildings until his retirement.

The newly created space soon proved to be inadequate to house the growing school. Outdoor classrooms which opened into the garden were created when every available space was covered and utilised for teaching: the corridor in front of the school building, the walkway to the north of the old garage, the new garage, and the coveted veranda at the front of the house was utilised once again. Some parents may not have been used to these unconventional teaching spaces, but staff and students preferred the cool breezes of outdoor teaching and learning. Retractable awnings were installed as a cover for the afternoon sun and the occasional shower of rain.

*

The first students were the children of close friends of the family, but Merrivale would eventually welcome students from across the globe, causing one student to think of the school as "the united nations." Apart from Barbados, there were students from several countries in the Caribbean: Anguilla, Haiti, Jamaica, St Vincent and the Grenadines and Trinidad and Tobago; South America: Guyana, Chile and Venezuela; North America, United States and Canada; Europe: United Kingdom, Belgium, Denmark and Norway; Asia, India and Malaysia; and Ghana, on the African continent.

The school was not only a mix of different nationalities and ethnicities, but also different religions; among them Christians, Hindus, Jews and Muslims. No group was elevated above the other. They were taught to respect each other; they mixed socially and developed special bonds with their peers as well as their teachers. At the end of Ramadan, a month-long period of fasting, reflection and prayer, the children of the Muslim faith brought cookies which they shared with their teachers and their peers. One student, who taught at the Alfalah School for Muslim children, continued to use her grammar notes from Merrivale, and credits "Teacher" with insisting that children speak standard English, a practice she also adopted.

In a quiet moment, when reflecting on her venture, from cautious initiative to expansion, and success, Avis chanced upon this verse from Henry Wadsworth Longfellow's "The Black Smith":

> Toiling, rejoicing, sorrowing,
> Onward through life he goes;
> Each morning sees some task begin,
> Each evening sees it close
> Something attempted, something done,
> Has brought a night's repose.

The poem speaks of hard work and dedication; it speaks of sorrow, but also of rejoicing. The line "Something attempted, something done," was chosen as the school motto; it served as a reminder of her journey and was a source of inspiration for teachers and students alike.

SEVEN

"There is no magic to achievement. It's really about hard work, choices and persistence." —Michelle Obama

Mrs Carrington and the teaching staff of Merrivale(1995 - 1996).
Front row from left: Mrs Margaret Rock, Ms Antoinette Williams,
Mrs Avis Carrington and Mrs Caroline Clarke. Back row from
left:
Ms Natalie Knight, Mrs Ardith Snagg, Ms Sandra Cumberbatch,
Ms Beverly Jones, and Mrs Jennifer Holder.

Something Done Well

AVIS Carrington and her staff worked assiduously, with an intense commitment to excellence; yet, she was amazed at the progress the school had made in its short history. Ever reluctant to take credit, she paid tribute to the students for being the "true creators of the school." They had "inspired" and "spurred" her on with "zeal and passion, necessary in the teaching profession." And she commended her "awesome staff for their loyalty and dedication". The occasion was the fortieth anniversary of Merrivale's opening. The sentiment was reciprocated when the teachers, students and their parents identified Avis Carrington, teacher and founder, as the principal reason for the school's success.

She was the cornerstone on which the school was built. Firmly grounded in education theory from her training at Erdiston, and the instructional skills honed through years of teaching at the primary level, she served with integrity and humility. Her vision of education placed the child at the centre of the teaching and learning process. The title "headmistress," which would later become "principal," was seldom used to address her, except for formal correspondence. The staff addressed her as Mrs Carrington and to the students, she was simply "Teacher," the most fitting title, because this was her first love and passion, the one most dear to her heart.

Her philosophy of education was evident in the aims and objectives of the school. The primary goal was to strive for scholastic excellence and to assist students in realising their full potential. Physical fitness and healthy habits were promoted, and moral and spiritual development were encouraged through the tenets of the Christian faith. Teachers were also reminded of their responsibility in moulding the life and character of each of their students. Most importantly, the administration and staff of the school were expected to demonstrate a loving concern for each child. The statement, "Profit is not the driving force behind the operation of Merrivale Preparatory School," concluded the stated list of goals.

Merrivale was much more than the building, teaching and a set of rules. Gardening was Avis' hobby, and she transformed the landscape to a welcoming collage of calming greens accentuated with an array of colour and charm that reflected her character; a fitting backdrop for the culture of the school. The ethos, though intangible, was visible everywhere; it embodied her generosity and compassion, her decorum and her grace. It was in the cordial interactions among staff, teachers, students, parents and visitors to the school. It was in the shared goals and the established norms and values, and sung in the songs, and repeated in the prayers that asked for God's blessings, and thanked Him for "The world so sweet, the food we eat, the birds that sing, and everything."

Avis Carrington was the founder and architect of things instructional, but she saw her husband Vere, a senior civil servant, as the real hero of Merrivale. Vere Carrington was a magistrate, a Registrar of the Supreme Court, and he rose to the highest rank of Permanent Secretary in the Ministry of Home Affairs. In 1966, at age fifty, Vere retired from the Civil Service and practised law at Cottle Catford & Co.; later he was appointed Queen's Counsel. Yet, he managed the overall operations of the school and home, making sure that both were maintained in good order.

The cost was high, but Avis insisted that the property was spruced up to welcome the new school year. Any damages were repaired and walls were repainted. The concrete floor of the open spaces was covered with linoleum to reduce the dust level and created another problem, a slippery surface. Vinyl tiles were cheaper and easier to replace, and not as smooth as linoleum. A pillar that supported the roof was wrapped in thick rope to soften any impact should a child bump into it. Any sign of unravelling and the design was quickly restored.

Vere was committed to supporting Avis in her venture and ensured that all requests were met. Vere's portfolio also included correspondence with the Ministry of Education and other agencies, and the procurement of teaching and other resources. He was also the accountant and payroll clerk. These tasks he did quietly and unobtrusively as was his nature.

From the beginning, Avis set about creating the nurturing classroom she yearned for as a child in elementary school. The numbers were small in the early years, and she taught all students until an increase in enrolment required the employment of additional staff. The recruitment of quality teachers was critical to maintaining what she envisioned for the school; from the Montessori methods and her on-the-job training she would adopt mentoring as an effective way of passing on valuable knowledge and skills.

As a result, she focused on a love for children, a passion for teaching and a positive attitude when selecting staff. These were favoured over certification and years of teaching. The trainee teachers came straight from secondary school; seven from the early seventies came from Springer Memorial School. Through their on-the-job training, the recruits soon embraced the vision she had for the school, developed into quality teachers, and maintained a culture of academic excellence.

Pat Byer, Avis' niece, was the first hired teacher. She was fresh out of Washington High School, a coeducational private school that provided schooling at the secondary level at a time when places were limited in the public system, especially for girls. These schools flourished until the government provided universal access for all students at that level. When Pat moved to the United States, she recommended her school friend Beverly Herbert, who taught art and writing to the kindergarten students. After her in-house training, arithmetic and English were added to her portfolio.

Gloria Watson (née Gittens), Hazel Busby, Patricia Bedford (née Mottley), Hazel Prescod and Isill Messiah joined the staff in the early sixties. The school was in its infancy, and these teachers helped to lay the foundation for the quality school that Merrivale became. Hazel Busby remembered a warm and welcoming Mrs Carrington. "Our hearts met from the very beginning." She echoed the thoughts of her colleagues who thought that Merrivale was a very special place to work, and they were grateful that they were given the opportunity. Ms Busby spent a total of three years before a transfer to a career in childcare, which was her first love.

Ms Bedford spoke highly of the school and of Mrs Carrington in particular. "She was great. She was a good mix of friendly and strict and stuck to manners and principles. She valued punctuality and brought out the best in students and teachers alike. She was caring and saw to it that teachers sat with the youngest children and made sure that they ate lunch."

Avis was indebted to all those who taught at Merrivale, some for a short time; Betty Wharton spent three years, Sandra Jones two and Karen Bostic one term. Former students also interned at the school; Karen Applewhaite, Kimberly Peters, Kheri Carrington, Maureen Ward, Natalie Knight and Nicole Edghill. This was Teacher in the role of mentor, assisting members of the Merrivale family who had shown an interest in teaching.

Avis is especially grateful to those teachers who sacrificed a larger salary and opportunities for promotion in the public service to make a long-term commitment to Merrivale. When the school closed in 2010, four of the five remaining teachers had each spent over thirty-five years there. This length of dedication meant that the climate of the school was maintained and easily passed on to generations of students.

Jennifer Holder was the most senior member of staff with thirty-eight years at Merrivale. Apart from her role as the teacher of Class 3, she deputised for Mrs Carrington on occasions and represented the school at meetings held at the Ministry of Education. She was trusted as a confidante with whom pressing matters were shared. She assumed the role of protector and shielded Mrs Carrington from bothersome routine issues or minor complaints, choosing to inform her after the problem was resolved.

Avis knew that Beverly Jones had a gentle voice and easy nature; she was sought out when students were in trouble and her corner became a place of refuge. She had an eye for detecting potential problems and could defuse a situation with an invitation to join her for a little chat. Students remembered her with fondness: many of them remained in contact with their "favourite teacher" for years afterward.

Margaret Rock was talented in the field of arts and craft and, with Caroline Clarke, taught the subject throughout the school. These skills were on full display when decorating for special events, and the school's art exhibition. Mrs Rock's expertise in calligraphy was used to prepare shields and scrolls for graduation. She was also the teacher of the Transition Class, a group of fast-track five-year-olds mixed with children as old as seven.

Mrs Carrington touted the thoroughness of her infant programme, thanks to Antoinette Williams, who was especially gifted with the

Reception class of four-year-olds. She allowed new students their quirks until they were mature enough to adopt the norms of the classroom. One student preferred to work from under the desk, and that was exactly where she sat, until she "grew out of it." Miss Williams enjoyed teaching at that level and used various methods, including outdoor activities, field trips and projects.

Some teachers moved on but not before making a significant contribution to the school. When Ardith Snagg (née Collins) retired in 1999 to take care of her mother, she had been a member of staff for twenty-seven years. Like her colleagues, Mrs Snagg was fresh out of high school and was hired as a floating teacher to assist in the team-teaching format. After her in-house training, she was first assigned to Reception and then transferred to Class 1. She was inspired by her mentor who "had the knack for analysing and diagnosing children. She stuck to the task until each student understood." Mrs Snagg was also skilled at helping children to settle down, especially little boys, who tended to be restless.

Sandra Cumberbatch (née Davis) spent seventeen years and was a very active participant in the extra-curricular programme. For eight years Caroline Clarke made a significant contribution in the area of arts and craft. They were later employed in the public service. The last four remaining teachers easily found employment at private primary schools when Merrivale closed its doors.

Avis Carrington was an instructional specialist in her own right and utilised practices from her own teaching at St Giles' Boys'. Like her mentor Mr Cumberbatch, she paired new teachers with more experienced teachers. She demonstrated methods, observed teaching skills and provided feedback. Apart from her role of teacher of Class 4 and Class 5, she taught each class in the school, while the class-teacher observed and assisted.

Teaching skills were further enhanced when staff pursued additional training, either from the Ministry of Education workshops or when they took advantage of the Easter programmes at Erdiston Teachers' Training College. The courses offered were Early Childhood Education, Reading, Mathematics, Poetry, and Dance. The whole staff also benefitted from the practice of team teaching and the sharing of resources. This method proved to be very effective, especially in mixed-ability groups in which each child received assistance according to his or her needs. With no physical barriers between classes, teachers also learned by observing one another.

Like most classrooms in public and private schools, "chalk and talk" was the dominant teaching method at Merrivale. However, with increased training, teachers incorporated modern methods, like portfolios, projects, field trips and tours, with tried and tested ones, like the use of a double-lined book for writing skills, flash cards, rote learning, repetition of the times tables, and other drills. Dictation was avoided; memories of nervous children trembling in fear, and not being able to keep up with the pace of the teacher, spared the Merrivale students from this method of assessment.

While acknowledging that mechanical repetition does not necessarily promote higher forms of thinking, Avis used rote learning to train young minds to store and retrieve information. This provided a foundation of knowledge on which other domains of learning, comprehension, analysis, synthesis, and evaluation were developed. One student recalled how "the unforgettable teaching of the 'rule of three' helped in navigating the intricacies of maths into secondary school and through university." This was a drill that required a three-line statement when solving mathematical problems.

Most importantly, Teacher stressed the importance of being thorough and methodical and encouraged students to aim for perfection in their writing. Compositions, or essays, had to be written over and over until all spelling and grammatical errors were corrected before they were transcribed into a special exercise book used for that purpose. The notation "CB" for composition book, written in bold print, was received with enthusiasm; this meant that there were no errors. Those receiving a CB underlined with red ink had to correct minor errors. Students without the coveted letters willingly sacrificed part of their playtime to reach the required standard. This was not seen as punishment; the children were eager to be counted among those who had successfully completed the task.

In a departure from the rigid approach to teaching, where children were not allowed to question the teacher, or deviate from the one method taught to solve a problem, students were taught problem-solving skills and encouraged to be creative when finding solutions. Antonio Rowe, former student and now a civil engineer, explained the benefit of this approach to problem-solving. "Mrs Carrington ensured that not only could you solve a problem but understood it so critically that you could solve it in any form and in any direction."

Testing was used to determine student progress and the results were communicated to parents. Mrs Carrington was mindful that reports should speak exactly to the progress of each child in each subject. It should be thorough and include remarks on all the cognitive and psychomotor abilities. The parent should be left with no doubt about the development of the child. She was "horrified" when she saw a report from one of the leading secondary schools. "What did 'fair,' 'good' and 'only fair' really mean?" she queried. In contrast, a report for a child in the reception class at Merrivale spoke about the child's ability with writing: "Can make strokes but has not mastered curves." For another student who had a reading problem, "Experiencing difficulty reading but makes a laudable effort". No report left the school without Mrs Carrington's oversight and approval.

Underpinning the technical aspects of teacher training was the special relationship Avis had with her staff. Caroline Clarke, who taught at Merrivale, still considers herself one of the best teachers on the island, "without apologies". She prides herself on her ability to prepare a written progress report for each child in the class; this skill she learned from her mentor, and one that she readily shared with her colleagues at Workman's Primary School.

"She was not only the 'principal' of Merrivale Preparatory School, but she was also, to me, a mother, mentor, an advisor, educator; humble by nature, a nurturer of children, approachable, and positive in her daily interaction with her students and staff," said Mrs Clarke. "When I am asked about different strategies of teaching, I always return to the memories of Mrs Carrington's modelling or discussing with me how a subject should be taught."

*

By the time Merrivale's first students were ready for transfer to secondary school, admission had shifted from just those who could afford to pay, to those who had the aptitude to pass the common entrance exam. By 1959, the exam was a two-part test taken by all ten-year-old children. A pass in Part 1, the screening test, secured entry to Part 2, which was administered by the grammar school to which the child was trying to gain access. Students were afforded a second chance to write the exam at age eleven. Those who did not gain a place at a grammar school were automatically assigned to a predetermined comprehensive school for which the primary school in its area served as a feeder school.

The academic programme is dictated by the national curriculum, which contains elements of each of the major areas of study. However, there was a perception that primary education was severely compromised, especially at levels three and four, where the emphasis was placed largely on English and mathematics, the only two subjects tested in the common entrance exam. But Avis Carrington was steadfast in her belief that children who acquired a broader range of knowledge would be better prepared for secondary education and life in general. In addition to the core subjects, the programme at Merrivale included art and craft, drama, physical education, games, singing, music, library and, later, computer studies. After the common entrance exam, students were introduced to basic French.

Up until 2019, the majority of primary students wrote a single exam when reaching age eleven by the first of September of the academic year in which the test was taken. The score on this exam, along with the parent's choice of school and the zone in which the child lived determined the secondary school the child attended.

To achieve maximum benefit for each student, an alternative method of grouping children was used at Merrivale. Students in Reception were admitted at age four, one year earlier than in public schools. The age of the child was not rigidly enforced as in public schools, instead, fast-track five-year-olds were promoted from Reception to the Transition Class. This group included students from Infants A with an age range from five to seven. This method of sorting allowed students to reach Class 4 at age 10, one year earlier than the public school. At age eleven, students were then promoted to Class 5, where they took the common entrance exam.

Children worked at their own pace until they mastered the required skills, and most children benefitted from the additional year. Fast-paced students worked ahead, and reached the exam class early, affording them more time to master the curriculum. Unfortunately, the education policy of the day prevented these gifted children from writing the exam before they reached age eleven. Mia Mottley was forced to wait two years before writing the exam. One of her signature policies as Minister of Education, Youth Affairs and Culture was Flexible Transfer. Introduced in the reforms of the 1995 White Paper on Education, it allows students to transfer to secondary school as early as age nine, or as late as thirteen.

Under the leadership of Avis Carrington, Merrivale soon earned a reputation for sound academic grounding, a disciplined environment, smaller classes, a feeling of community, and individual attention. It was ranked among the top schools that offered the best chances for admission to the coveted grammar schools, with their long histories of tradition and academic excellence. The school population at the highest ranked secondary schools is skewed in favour of the upper and middle classes; these are the families that can afford to pay for a private education. This method of allocation is perceived as elitist, because those who are already privileged see themselves as more deserving because of their special skills, ability and status.

The Shorey Report of 1974 examined the transfer of students from primary to secondary school in Barbados to address these issues, especially the distinction that existed between the grammar and the comprehensive schools. To improve the public image of comprehensive schools, they were added to the list of schools from which parents could make their choices. The terms "grammar" and "comprehensive" were discontinued in favour of "Government Secondary Schools," the current designation for all public schools at that level. In addition, Partial Zoning, an initiative of the reforms of 1995, was implemented to encourage a greater spread of students across the secondary schools. Despite these efforts, the former grammar schools continue to sit at the top of a hierarchical positioning of secondary schools in the island.

*

Avis Carrington was not a fan of this time of the year. It was the month of May, and parents and their children awaited the dreaded common entrance exam, with mixed feelings of excitement, uncertainty, anxiety and fear. The hype associated with the results had become an annual media event when the top scorers and their schools were celebrated. For those who failed to make the grade, sometimes missing a favoured school by a few marks, there was disappointment, sometimes punishment and tears; and a label that persisted with some children for the rest of their lives. Not only did they carry the burden of having let their parents down but were cloaked in a uniform that was an announcement of their failure at age eleven. Children with cognitive and social issues who made progress, and their teachers who persevered, were seldom mentioned.

For Avis Carrington this was personal. "While they are shedding tears, I am shedding too," she shared. She knew of her struggles at the primary level and understood that the exam was stressful and that some children did not perform at their best when tested. As a result, their comfort was given top priority when preparing for the exam. Students practised for the test, but they were not confined to repetitive practice on past papers ad infinitum. The exam was treated as just another test at a different location, with just one imposition: after one week of the three-week Easter vacation, Class 5, the exam class, returned to school for extra lessons at no additional cost to parents. After the test, the children were treated to Kentucky Fried Chicken, or pizza, until educational trips with a fun element became the norm.

If Avis Carrington had been given responsibility for education policy, she would have abolished the entrance exam with its ranking and rating; and recommend instead monitoring, assessing and the use of remediation when necessary. This was the preferred method at Merrivale; children were tested weekly at class level to make sure that each child met the required standard of achievement. In addition, students across the school looked forward to a spelling quiz every Friday morning.

Teacher spent time with each class throughout the week, observing, mentoring, teaching, and testing. As a result, she could speak to the academic progress of every child in the school. Those who were not achieving at the required rate were identified and given additional assistance. It was not unusual to see staff hurrying lunch to make time to assist a child who had fallen behind. This was not a requirement; teachers had seen Mrs Carrington's commitment to slower learners. The underlying assertion was clear and definitive and teachers followed her lead; "Can't is not an acceptable excuse at Merrivale. It is the teacher's responsibility to make sure that children understand the principles: if not today, tomorrow." "Reading is a must. You have to learn to read."

The accomplishment of which Avis was most proud was the progress of those who struggled to grasp concepts, yet exceeded expectations. She had compassion for, and was committed to these students: the child who competently presented the vote of thanks after experiencing difficulty with reading, the student who was transferred from a prestigious private school because he was not making progress and is now a medical doctor; these she saw as Merrivale's success stories.

Mandatory screening for sight, speech and hearing impairment was still in the future, and the word dyslexia was not yet common in the local education discourse. With no formal training in the field of diagnostic testing, Avis had to rely on her instincts and knew in her heart when a child needed an intervention. Alternative teaching methods were first tried by the class teacher, and in cases when little or no improvement resulted, the child was selected for special one-on-one coaching. She understood the need for sensitivity and tact when informing parents. Fortunately, they trusted her judgment and consented to the suggested routine.

A spirit of caring and sharing was already the norm at Merrivale, making it easy to involve the whole school when a child needed help. When new students joined the school family, they were greeted with a hug, and each student was assigned a "big brother" or "sister"; some students needed the support more than others.

"I was traumatised."

It was Mark's first day at school. Finally, he was at this "magical big school" his older brother Paul boasted about. On arriving he was met with stares of what felt like one hundred children, who were taller and bigger and louder than he was. All was fine until his big brother left him at the start of the school day. Mark bawled his eyes out. He cried for his brother, his mother, and declared that he had had enough of school and wanted to go home.

A senior girl, watching Mark's meltdown, volunteered to be his "big sister." Charmaine sat with him on the veranda, a safe distance from the gigantic children with loud voices and glaring eyes, and busied him with light chatter, drawing and colouring. Soon Mark had settled. Throughout the day, she checked with him, and was there during lunch break to make sure he ate all his lunch. By the second day, Mark was in his class, but Charmaine continued to monitor his progress until he made new friends. Mark cherished this friendship, and she became the big sister he never had, and a lifelong friend.

Mark was not the only one who suffered from first day blues. Mia Mottley was not yet four when she started school at Merrivale, and refused to join her class for a whole week. Instead, she followed Teacher around until two senior girls were assigned to help her settle. "If that first week had been handled differently?" she questioned. "What would be the consequences of the kind of person I might have become? There was the nurturing, the understanding that I needed; that I could move at my own pace."

In this climate, children readily participated in peer tutoring. First, Teacher explained that each child was different, some with unique talents, and needs; a timid child may require encouragement, another may have difficulty reading or solving mathematical problems. Rather than bullying or laughing at a child who needed help, students readily offered to assist their classmates, which proved to be beneficial to both students. The volunteer student reinforced his or her own learning, developed feelings of empathy and won the admiration of teachers and classmates. The student being supported experienced improvement in his or her academic achievement, which built confidence; and both students realised a boost in self-esteem through their respective roles.

*

The dining room where the first students gathered in 1959 was the meeting place for special sessions with Teacher. Avis preferred a 7 a.m. start to coach students, but for those who needed to adequately grasp a lesson that was taught earlier in the day, after-school sessions were the norm; and Teacher thought nothing of rushing lunch to be with a student. She spent a considerable amount of time on individual coaching, and boys were more likely than girls to need tutoring. However, over the years she had not observed a gender difference in the common entrance exam results at Merivale. A likely explanation is that boys who fell behind their female peers were caught in the ongoing cycle of assessment and remediation before they took the exam.

"When she noticed that one of my boys was possibly dyslexic, she mentioned it to me without fanfare and determined to use a strategy whereby he would be in no way made uncomfortable among his peers or lose confidence in himself," recalls Ann (now Lady) Hewitt, a noted educator, adding that Avis' handling of this situation was "nothing less than brilliant." Teacher worked around the problem by engaging the boy's strengths. He was good at math and she allowed him to teach Venn diagrams to his clasmates. This boosted his confidence; he was able to compensate for the impediment, earn a 90% performance and a place at Harrison College in the 11-plus examination.

Another mother shared her son's transformational experience. He was withdrawn from one of the top public primary schools when she realised that, at age seven, he was unable to read. She sought out private schooling, but his diagnosis of dyslexia caused him to be turned away

99

by several schools. In desperation, she turned to Merrivale after hearing about the reputation of the school from a close friend. The mother acknowledged that her son had a learning problem and asked only that he acquire basic levels of literacy and numeracy; she assumed that the common entrance exam was beyond his capability. Mrs Carrington was reluctant. At age eight, he was one year older than the upper limit she had set for enrolment; and she feared that missing the expertise of Miss Williams and her infant methods would place him at a disadvantage.

Each morning before school started, Teacher spent time transforming this boy's life. He was given responsibility that boosted his self-esteem, and soon he became very popular with his peers and was fully integrated into the school. Working at his own pace, he gradually improved, and three years later, he successfully completed the common entrance exam and was transferred to a public secondary school, where he became a senior prefect. Later, he enrolled in a post-secondary institution and completed an internship with a business, which was a requirement of his programme. He was dedicated and skilled, had a good work ethic, and was eventually appointed to a permanent position in the government service.

Assigning tasks to children to make them responsible was a core value of the school. It was seen as part of their education, with the additional benefit of developing their self-worth, and according to several students, "making us who we are today." Throughout the life of the school, students shared in preparing the teaching areas. Small chairs and tables were lifted and shifted, easels were set up and blackboards were cleaned and mounted. Some students packed the drinks machine with glass bottles of Coke, Frutees and Sprite, while one select student transported the coin box to the house when it was full. A very important assignment was pencil monitor; this student shared the writing tools at the start of the class and ensured that each was collected at the end of the day. But the most prestigious of all was the ringing of the bell to start the school day. And all students were reminded to keep their surroundings clean and tidy while reciting this rhyme from *The Child Education Magazine* to which the school subscribed:

> If you see paper on the ground
> Don't let it blow away.
> Pick it up
> Pop it in
> Drop it in the litter bin.

While children would be children and get into mischief, the mood of the school was calm, warm and kind. Children were taught to be accepting of others, to assist their peers, to be responsible and to exercise self-discipline. Everyone was treated the same, "simply special," regardless of colour, religion, financial status, or level of academic ability. Students were encouraged to support each other and to share, led by the example of their teachers who were always willing to assist. As a result, those who visited Merrivale noted that it stood out among other schools.

*

The education process is dynamic, and Avis has seen a lifetime of changes. She was already a teacher when Grantley Adams, the first premier of Barbados, held the education portfolio. She witnessed the appointment of Luther Thorne, the first Minister of Education, under ministerial government, and the first female, when Billie Miller became Minister of Education in 1985. She celebrated the appointment of former student Mia Mottley in 1994, the second female and youngest at twenty-eight to hold that post. With each change of government, the Ministry of Education assumed a new title, which often reflected changes in policy. In order to ensure continual success, the school had to keep pace with these reform initiatives. Together with the staff, Mrs Carrington determined which trends were fleeting and which were best fitted to the needs of Merrivale Preparatory School.

The school kept pace through an ongoing relationship with the ministry which is ultimately responsible for the education of each child in the nation. For several of its initiatives, Merrivale was already ahead of the curve. By the time the child-centred philosophy, awareness of social and emotional learning, and attainment targets for each student were implemented, they had already been part of the policy and practice of the school.

Avis and her staff also kept current by sourcing the latest literature and other resources, like films and education journals. The Child Education Magazine was produced for teachers of nursery to primary-age children. It provided rich, timely infusions of creative ideas underpinned by education theory and was the source of the school prayer. It was published by Evans Brothers Ltd. and sold locally by Mr Todd on Swan Street in Bridgetown.

Some reforms were challenging for a small private school. One was the Education Sector Enhancement Programme, or EduTech, launched in 1997. The five main objectives were to repair public schools, to provide teacher training, to achieve a balance between teacher-centred and child-centred education, to strengthen the capacity of the ministry to manage the education system, and to integrate information and communications technology (ICT) into the school system.

Operating on a limited budget, the school was unable to effect the structural changes thought necessary to accommodate the technology. But this was not seen as a deterrent. Forty-eight years after graduating from Erdiston Teachers' Training College, Avis returned to be schooled in the integration of the ICT programme to ready Merrivale for Education Reform 2000. The school was selected as one of the first private primary schools to benefit from EduTech resources when it acquired two computers with assistance from the Ministry of Education.

Some reform proposals were home-grown. The extracurricular programme was a collaborative effort between teachers and parents, and it was received with great enthusiasm by the students. This resulted in the expansion of the curriculum to include activities that enhanced fitness and health, fostered creativity, and developed social skills. Part of the success of this initiative was the enthusiastic support from parents.

One should never underestimate the impact of parental involvement and Merrivale was fortunate to have the backing of parents from its inception. As the school expanded and evolved, greater structure and organisation was brought to the parent body and the Merrivale Parent Teacher Association (PTA) was established. This started a tradition of joint initiatives with the parents: the annual school fair, the graduation ceremony and sports day. One of the chief architects of this initiative was Hilford Murrell, who rallied the parents and teachers. Tony Reece was elected the first president in 1982. Stafford Martin, Lionel Sealy, James Linton, Rory Hunte, Ms St John and Dale Foster all served in the post. Dale Foster was the last president, and her daughter Kabira was one of the last five students to graduate from Merrivale. Apart from her dedicated service, she made a personal donation to the school at a time when the revenue from tuition fees was in decline.

Parents maintained standards by making their concerns known. Graduates spoke highly of Merrivale and their children also became students of the school. Many parents sought Mrs Carrington for transfers when their children were not making progress at other schools. Despite the dedication of Mrs Carrington and her staff, some parents were not pleased with the concept of the rounded student, preferring more emphasis on subjects tested in the common entrance exam. Some children were sent to lessons, and others were withdrawn. One of the complaints in the later years was Teacher's age. These concerns became more frequent in the last year of the school, as parents grappled with the imminent closure. The staff resolved matters where possible, knowing how much she had sacrificed to maintain the school, and shielded her from many of these complaints.

Mrs Carrington was always quick to praise her staff. On the fortieth anniversary of the school, she expressed her appreciation for the teachers in a short address: "I could not have accomplished this awesome task alone," she noted. "So, it is with deep gratitude that I salute my staff for their loyalty and dedication." She again echoed her admiration and appreciation for her staff in a Government Information Service documentary, *We Bajans*, 2018. "Many people speak about Miss Carrington School, but I could not have run this school alone." Dan, herself an educator, acknowledged her sister's commitment to the school, but was mindful of the role of the staff. "She worked hard, she worked very hard, and she was able to attract very good teachers."

Mrs Carrington's mantra, "Hard work and commitment produce good rewards," set the tone for the work ethic, and the staff exceeded what was required of them. They were not only accomplished in the mastery of their designated roles as teachers; in collaboration with parents they initiated, planned and coordinated several of the activities in the extra-curricular programme that further enhanced the character of the school. In addition, the teachers at Merrivale exhibited a loyalty that was seldom seen at other schools, public or private. They shared Mrs Carrington's love for the school and were entirely committed to the progress of the children in their care.

EIGHT

"We must remember that intelligence plus character, that is the goal of true education." —Martin Luther King, Jr

Cub Scout leader Jacqueline Mottley and Merrivale Cub Scouts stand at attention during a drill routine. Girls were allowed to participate.

A Well-rounded
Student

WHEN Avis Carrington founded Merrivale, scholastic excellence was the primary goal of the school. Of equal significance was the physical, moral and spiritual development of the child; the goal, to produce a well-rounded happy child. The school prayer captures the spirit of Merrivale, and everyone joined in to give thanks:

> For food and flowers and happy hours
> And love that cares for me
> For all the joys of girls and boys
> We give our thanks to thee.

With Mrs Carrington's blessings, keen students, teachers and parents invested their time, talents, money and other resources that led to the success of the extracurricular programme. The activities, several of which were inspired by *The Child Education Magazine*, readily lent themselves to singing, drama and dance, which were on show at the end-of-term parties. In more formal sessions, the whole school joined in the breathing exercises and sang along with the "education through radio" programming on Barbados Rediffusion Service Limited. This was a wired broadcasting system that introduced radio to the island in the 1930s.

In the 1950s, radio education programming started when the service was installed in public places, like primary schools across the island. The sessions were directed by the late Canadian-born Doris Provençal, who moved to Barbados in 1952 when she married John Kirton, a Barbadian. She also taught music at Foundation Girls' School, Harrison College and St Gabriel's School. The mezzo-soprano founded the Festival Choir and the Cecilian Singers and contributed to the tradition of choral groups in her adopted home.

Vocal expertise was not a requirement for these activities; the aim was to have the whole school join in, sing lustily and make a joyful noise.

The children gathered around a vintage radiogram, a small wooden cabinet with a built-in record player. They sat and listened attentively and wrote the words to their favourite tunes in their song books: "A Whale," "Catch a Falling Star," "Chitty Chitty Bang Bang," "Did You Ever See a Lassy?," "Jimmy Crack Corn," "Seems," "Tipperary," "Up on the Housetop," "When I First Came to the Land," and "Zip-a dee-doo-dah." Singing, which was an essential part of the curriculum back then, would eventually be used only at morning assembly and for end-of-term parties.

The younger Carrington son was hopeless at singing. Ian had not inherited the gift from his parents, who could both "hold a tune." He was fortunate to have the renowned Ms Provençal as his music teacher at secondary school. With her skills, she could rectify any musical deficiency, his mother thought. A reluctant Ian made little progress and was quick to admit that he just could not sing.

"Everyone can sing," the tutor countered. "In all of my years in music, I've met only one little girl at the Girls' Foundation School who could not sing." "Exactly ma'am" was the quick reply. "It runs in the family. That girl is my sister."

Ian also failed miserably at piano. All he knew was the stained chipped keys of Ms Arthur's old piano boldly marked with letters to help the students memorise the names and location of the keys; but this strategy proved to be futile. How was he to remember the notes when on the day of the exam, the piano had been upgraded to a polished instrument with pristine ivory coated keys with not a letter in sight?

On special occasions like Christmas, end-of-term parties and graduation ceremonies, the school came alive with the sound of music, dance and drama. Staff, students, parent volunteers and family members prepared the actors for their various roles. Brightly coloured crêpe paper was cut, cinched, taped and sewn together and, later, leotards and tights and oversized clothing transformed the cast into dainty little dancers, Santa and his busy elves, or Mary, Joseph and the three wise men.

Avis was so committed to this programme that she sought the assistance of trained personnel. Ramoun Joseph, the dance tutor, came to the school highly recommended by a parent and did not disappoint. He choreographed the routine for the seasonal productions and had everyone on their toes. When her four-year old daughter was enrolled in 2001, Sharon Grant immediately volunteered her services. The school could not afford the expense of full-time instructors, but weekly dance classes were subsidised, allowing students to pay a minimal fee. The investment in dance was rewarded when the school's troupe won bronze at the National Independence Festival of Creative Arts (NIFCA).

Art and craft, also called handicraft, was taught to all students. Some parents volunteered their services, teaching students who were eager to learn. The art gallery was merely a small corner, but drawings and paintings framed with brightly coloured Bristol board were proudly displayed; and the pompoms, garlands and streamers made their way to special events as party decorations. Several students shared how art and craft at Merrivale influenced their lives and was the stimulus that sparked a lifelong interest in the subject: "She made colour blossom in my heart." "The love of art flourished." "It became my passion."

*

Avis Carrington understood the importance of physical education as well as the benefits of free play. The paved yard at the front provided a hard surface for cricket, jump rope and hopscotch and a parcel of land at Erdiston, Pine Hill, which was owned by the Crown, and conveniently located adjacent to the raised area at the back of the property, was leased and used as a playground. The space was not ideal, and resources were limited, but children participated enthusiastically, either in spontaneous play or more formal physical education sessions. An official sports day was launched by sports enthusiast Sandra Davis, now Cumberbatch, in collaboration with the newly formed PTA.

Sports day brought back fond memories of participating in athletics at secondary school, and Avis spared no effort to ensure the event was a success. Red, Yellow and Blue Houses participated in friendly rivalry with enthusiastic cheerleaders chanting in support; the uniforms were designed and made by one of the parents, Sandra (Sandie) Field. The event was held on the grounds of sports clubs at Barclays, Banks Breweries or Barbados External Telecommunications Ltd., all in Wildey. Hector Edwards of the NSC, a former Olympic cyclist, served as chief judge and timer for the traditional track events.

The relays at the end of the meet were always highly anticipated; but the lime-and-spoon and three-legged races generated the most fun, especially when the lime parted company with the spoon, and two-headed bodies with "three" legs hopped, hobbled and tumbled their way to the finish line. The prize-giving ceremony was special, if not unique. Long before the debate on whether all students should be rewarded, each child at Merrivale received a small trophy for participation. These awards which recognised effort and determination were a boost to the self-confidence of those who would never win an event.

Avis Carrington was eager to expand the sports programme and established a working relationship with Jasper Blades of the NSC. He held a Diploma in Physical Education and a Master of Science in Sports Development and Administration. After negotiating the use of the playing field at Erdiston Teachers' Training College, he introduced cricket and football to the curriculum, causing the programme to be closer aligned to the public primary school. Merrivale did not compete in these sports, but individual students participated in the National Primary Schools' Athletic Championship (NAPSAC). Some went on to represent their secondary schools in the equivalent competition at that level, the Barbados Secondary Schools' Athletic Championships (BSSAC).

Mrs Carrington believed that children should learn life skills and self-discipline to help them become good citizens, ideals she shared with the Girl Guides Association of Barbados and the Barbados Boy Scouts Association. Units of these organisations could be found across government and private schools in Barbados. The age range was from seven to eleven for both groups, but there was a Beaver Scout Pack for boys, ages four to seven. The goals of the organisations were achieved through adherence to codes and pledges. In addition, members earned badges on the completion of prescribed tasks.

The cub scouts met on Thursday afternoons with Jacqueline Mottley the pack leader. The onsite activities attracted many students including girls who were never turned away. The pack enjoyed cookouts, fish fries, and local and overseas camps. Christopher Blenman was a keen cub scout who completed thirty-seven badges over a four-year period. A proud moment for the school was when he was selected for the National Scout Band to play the snare drum, thought to be the most important drum in the kit.

The Brownie Guide pack was started in the early sixties by the late Hazel Alleyne, mother of the late Stephen Alleyne, who was best known for the outstanding contribution he made to the administration of cricket, at both the national and regional level. In 1990, the small unit joined Unit 44, an existing pack at Pax Hill with guiders Hetty Stoute-Oni and Lilas Vaughan. As more students from Merrivale joined, the pack at Merrivale became Unit 108 and met at the school; Guider Erline Toppin replaced Ms Vaughan and Nykeba Oni volunteered.

The vibrant pack of brownies hosted parties, wrote, produced and performed dramatic skits. They camped at home and abroad, and on a trip to St Lucia, the girls were given opportunities to manage their own groups. In 1992, eight brownies achieved The Barbados Brownie Badge, the highest award a brownie could earn locally. The girls in Unit 108 were known for their work ethic, and all excelled at their schoolwork.

*

The consequences of all work and no play were well known by Avis. Remembering how much she loved the outdoors as a child and the restrictions her father placed on her, she overcompensated and allowed the children free rein; a few guidelines ensured safety and spared the garden which was out of bounds. At lunchtime and after school, the grounds came alive with the voices of cheerful children.

The land at the back of the school and the adjacent area provided students with a playground that had character. They roamed what seemed like a vast area of uneven ground with dense tropical shrubs, but dared not venture beyond the banana plants that led to a dark thicket at the far end of the field.

They avoided the mysterious gated house in the shade of the overgrown trees. It was owned by the Connell family, but from their limited view it stood there eerily silent with dark mottled shadows dancing on its weathered walls. The winding track that led to the house snaked through a wooded area behind the school building, ending in a lonely cul-de-sac.

Hiding places were everywhere: behind the trees that bordered the lot, the shadow of the school building, and among the colourful shrubs. This was their wild, wild west, where two historic adversaries met daily. Everyone wanted to be a cowboy; little did they know that the Indians were the good guys who were stubbornly defending their land, culture and heritage. The "pow pow" of the guns signalled that the cowboys were in hot pursuit, and the Indians fought back with the hissing sounds of mimed arrows. Those who were killed on the field were miraculously resurrected to fight until the school bell signalled the end of the battle.

The rise at the back of the school was a gentle slope, but to the children this was a giant hill and the ideal site for sliding down the grassy slope. A mound of sand left over from the construction project provided the right medium and gradient for the thrill of a ride. An edict from Teacher deeming the area and the activity to be dangerous, did not deter some brave boys and girls. With shoes mimicking skis, contorted bodies attempting to defy gravity sped downhill to the cheers of their admiring peers.

Games that were lively or energetic were not allowed before the start of the school day, and girls either read or played with dolls. Boys were not invited to these activities, or chose to stay away, but at lunch break they joined with the girls in jumping, skipping, and hula-hooping, at times with improvisations that suited their taste. Boys enhanced the traditional pace of jump rope by jumping with excessive speed and flair in what they dubbed a "pepper round."

The boys were banned when the rope was reduced to a weakened, fuzzy mess. Mark, who cried his eyes out on that first day, had settled into the big school and had grown into one of the tall students with staring eyes. He vowed retaliation and was determined to reclaim the lost territory. He and his squad acquired a new rope and introduced "Kung Fu skipping." The girls retreated to safer games like Chinese skip, and Simon says, while the boys happily punched, kicked and bruised each other in this high intensity version of the game.

Ring games like Miss Mary Mack and Brown Girl in a Ring were often accompanied by a combination of singing and coordinated hand movements, and some required a "go down to low town," a gyrating of the hips as the body was lowered always out of range of Teacher. Red rover, Simon says, rounders, jump rope, hopscotch, and red-light-green-light-one-two-three were the most popular. Jacks, the X and O game, also known as tic-tac-toe, name-place-animal-thing, and card games like suck-me-well, rummy and I-declare-war, were played on rainy days, or when children were banned from the playing area for infringing the rules.

*

If the boys avoided girly games like playing with dolls, the girls ignored the gender stereotypes and thought nothing of engaging the best boys in a game of pitching marbles. They either completed a course of holes while keeping opponents at bay in killer or knocked marbles out of a circle in a game of pool. The best players were those able to execute an accurate pitch with just the right amount of power with the flick of a thumb. The winner earned a stash of shiny marbles. The spoils could include opaque eggies, plain or coloured crystals, and cat's eyes with the characteristic insertion of colour in the centre. A large marble called a taw and the prized steelie, which was really a ball bearing, earned the owners bragging rights and elevated status.

But the game of cricket reigned supreme. It was the sixties, and the West Indies team was on its way to world domination. Cricketers were heroes, and the passion for the game across the region bordered on religious zeal. Different versions of the game were played everywhere, standing or kneeling with improvised bats and balls: on open pastures, on playing fields, on beaches, the middle of a broad street, a narrow alley, and even between houses, where a broken window often told the tale of an ambitious batsman who refused to allow the cramped space to limit his choice of shots.

Cricket was played in every schoolyard across Barbados, and Merrivale was no exception. The rules were altered to suit the circumstances. If the ball was struck over the wall, the player was given out, restricting the left-handed batsmen from playing shots on the leg-side. Every boy wanted to cover drive like Garfield Sobers, dubbed "The greatest cricketer on Earth or Mars" by iconic calypsonian the Mighty Sparrow, or bowl as fast as Wes Hall; both were knighted later for their contribution to the game.

Philip Nicholls and his best friend, Stephen Alleyne, were two young fans who would later serve in cricket administration at the local and regional levels. Every morning, they waited patiently by the school gate to get a glimpse of Seymour Nurse, a right-handed batsman, as he dropped off his twin daughters. The glory days have long gone, but the game persisted as the most popular until the innings at Merrivale came to an end in 2010.

For every game, there was a season. "To this day," Lisa Clarke wondered, "I do not know how or who was responsible for coordinating the games aspect of my school days, but the options of marbles, hopscotch, Chinese skip, regular skipping, cards, jacks, ring games, hula hoop and cricket all had seasons. No one ever brought cards to jacks season. The mystery continues."

*

Whether activities were structured and supervised by teachers or parents, or initiated and organised by the students, the behaviour was exemplary. The rules were never written, this was just part of the culture of the school. Teacher was strict, but her nature was warm and mother-ly, and the tone was not forbidding. She ensured that boundaries were observed without compromising the cheerfulness so important to the ethos of Merrivale.

Several parents were graduates and they passed on the school culture to their children who maintained the behavioural norms and lived up to the high expectations. Standard English, the official language, was spoken in measured tones and "Bajan," the local dialect, was discouraged. Avis was as shocked as the students who shared their secondary school experience; talking back to teachers, obscene language, and fighting were alien to Merrivale.

When rules were breached, each teacher took full responsibility and resolved any disciplinary issues without input from Mrs Carrington. Led by the head boy and head girl, the prefect body provided additional eyes and ears; and sometimes the whole class was invited to share their opinion on a disciplinary matter. She believed, "When children are made aware of what is required of them, they respond well to that type of guidance."

"Pencils down," Teacher would say to get the attention of everyone, "Now is that appropriate behaviour?" she would ask and pause for opinions. She believed that involving children in setting standards helped them to develop the practice of monitoring their own behaviour, and that of others, and reporting those who misbehaved.

"Please, Teacher," the boy said, "Cara is using inappropriate language."

"No, I did not," Cara said.

"Yes, you did."

"No, I did not."

"Wait a minute," Teacher intervened.

"Cara used inappropriate language," he repeated, this time stressing each syllable for emphasis.

"No, I did not," she reiterated, this time with defiance. "He said he would report me, and I said I don't give a damn."

"Well, in my books," Teacher said firmly, "that is inappropriate language."

A few young men in the making were sometimes recruited and given responsibility to ensure that protocols were observed. There was the case of the boy who was asked to monitor the "sandy slopes" to ensure that children did not use the space as a skating rink. Those who were not in compliance were reported and received the mandatory penalty, some "warm lashes." The "informant" was keen to police this "illegal" activity and earn the respect and admiration of his teachers, but his popularity soon dwindled among his classmates and they were eager to get revenge.

They did not have long to wait. The afternoon was sunny, and the sand was loose and dry and very inviting. Not even the most dependable student could resist the temptation. The team of conspiring peers applied the pressure, urging on their adversary with praises of his daring and skill. With loyalty to the school administration greatly diminished and the significance of his supervisory role now in question, he buckled. Before long, the boy was flying down the slope at an exhilarating pace, again and again and again. The excitement was infectious, and the schemers soon joined in the fun.

Early the next morning, the guilt-ridden lad arrived at school, strutting around as one with status. After all, he still had responsibility for monitoring the hill; but soon he would have to answer for his lapse in judgement. His classmates could not wait to deliver the summons.

"Haw haw," they taunted him in unison. "Teacher would like to see you!"

There was no office, Teacher sat at her desk in the open area, awaiting the arrival of the defendant, the strap clearly in view. The accused took what felt like a very long walk to reach the site of the trial, agonising over the events of the previous day. Teacher had put her trust and confidence in him, he thought, and he had let her down. Regretting his behaviour, he approached with lowered head; nevertheless, he was determined to defend himself and face the consequences. If lucky, he could walk away with a reprimand, or face a stiffer penalty, the mandatory lashes for this infringement.

"I am disappointed in you," she said firmly. "I put you in charge, and I am told that you were skating in the sand?"

"No, teacher," he said timidly.

"But why should they report you if you were not skating?"

But this was no average student. In a show of what was preparation for his future career, the accused presented a spirited defence.

"They are trying to get back at me," he pleaded. But the argument was not convincing.

"Your shoes look full of sand for one who was not in it," Teacher pointed out.

"That is natural wear and tear and laziness associated with not cleaning my shoes every day, Teacher," he countered.

The outcome of the case was sealed when the key witnesses failed to testify at the hearing, opting to stay away instead. They were equally guilty and would have implicated themselves when cross-examined.

*

At times, Avis resorted to her quick wit to bring a situation under control. Philip was a Tudor of the funeral home family of Ivy Main Road. His father delighted in taking him to school in a hearse, as a reminder of his source of income, much to the amusement of his peers who were relentless in their playful teasing. Philip's father did not stop driving his son to school, nor change the mode of transportation; instead he agreed to grant his son's request to drop him halfway along Pine Road and let him walk the remaining distance.

As friends would, an argument between Philip Tudor and Philip Nicholls soon escalated; over what, neither of them could recall, but Philip Tudor sought to bring an end to it.

"Drop dead," he snapped within earshot of Teacher.

"School is no place to be looking for business for your father," she said without hesitation. Her response generated waves of laughter, and the dispute was soon forgotten.

The established code of behaviour was sometimes tested, especially by boys. It was a boy who chased a ball across the street; boys who threw small juice boxes that went "pop" when they were run over, then shouted, "tyre burst" at the unsuspecting driver. Another boy caused a near panic when he took a crab on to the bus after a field trip to Folkestone Marine Park in St James. A short cut across the lawn to win a bet about who could reach the garage first, left a tangled mess of garden hose, and yet another boy calmly announcing, "I think my hand 'brek.'" And indeed, it was.

Mark shared his escapades with his peers. "Boys and rocks went together like biscuits and cheese." And he often found himself with those who "had an impulsive desire to aim chunks of limestone at any target they deemed suitable." Boys threw small rocks at girls, never to do any damage, just to get their attention. Rocks were thrown into the mango tree, at birds, at lizards, at monkeys, and they were aimed at each other, on one occasion drawing blood when a boy "wandered" into the path of the missile. A favourite target was the outhouse next door, especially when the handyman was using the facility.

The latrine's door was bombarded with rocks daily, until a diamond-shaped peephole was discovered at the front of the structure. With the correct angle and skill, a small stone could reach the inside. The competition was on, but success ended this test of their aim and dexterity when the angry handyman emerged with suspenders around his knees, cursing at the offenders. Mark's "men" were banned from the hill for a long, long time, but this did not curb their passion for rock throwing.

Avis Carrington was great with male students at St Giles' Boys', and felt strongly that teaching boys would be her preference; she was even a little apprehensive about teaching girls. It took time getting used to the idea, but eventually the pendulum swung the other way and she found the girls less challenging. When taught together, it became evident that boys were more likely than girls to have learning difficulties and problems with their behaviour. Boys tested her patience, and she contemplated a change in policy. At times, admission was restricted to male students who already had siblings at the school; but Merrivale always maintained a coeducational school population.

There were consequences for students who did not comply with the school's code of conduct. At Merrivale, disciplinary practices were typical for the times. The adage "spare the rod and spoil the child" was associated with Scripture and was often used to justify the use of corporal punishment, both in the home and school. Avis believed that administering "two or three lashes" had its place. She cautioned teachers; at times children need to be disciplined, but there was no need to be abusive or cruel. This method remained largely unchallenged in Barbados until the United Nations invoked the 1990 Convention on the Rights of the Child. Article 28 states in part that, "school discipline should be administered in a manner consistent with the child's human dignity".

*

In 2004, a CADRES (Caribbean Development Research Services) poll conducted on behalf of UNICEF (United Nations Children's Fund) to track public opinion on the matter of corporal punishment, 70% of those polled agreed that corporal punishment should continue in

Barbadian schools. Five years later only 50% of the population held that view. However, the percentage of persons arguing for its retention in the home had not changed considerably, falling from 80% to 74%. Prohibitions on corporal punishment in some countries and partial bans in others have sought to curb this practice and it continues to be a contentious issue. The role of flogging is now restricted to principals and senior teachers in public schools in Barbados.

Long before the UN initiative Mrs Carrington advised her teachers to be patient, to avoid shouting, and corporal punishment was discouraged. But conflicting reports suggest that "licks" were used sparingly or liberally, depending on the decade and on the source. Miss Busby, one of the teachers from the early sixties, was encouraged to "guide the student" who was having difficulty forming her letters rather than resort to lashes. When Miss Jones joined the staff in 1976 spanking was still discouraged. However, students told a different story:

"Play the fool, pay the price, a few lashes with the infamous strap."
"It was not allowed to catch cobwebs."
"It should be in a museum," stated another, without giving a reason.

The "weathered," "tattered" "infamous" strap was kept in a see-through bag that migrated to Teacher's lap as the day progressed, maybe to serve as a deterrent. It was "stretched out to its fullest length" and "left a lasting impact" on those who were flogged. Richard Sealy, former Minister of Tourism, did not consider himself a problem child. By his own estimation, "boys would be boys, and for most boys that was standard." "Out of love," he added. "I can still see the strap in my mind." Another former student admitted that she was not applying herself fully when Teacher saw that she could give more with a little help. "Ms Carrington saw in me something that I did not see in myself and unlocked my hidden academic with a little worn leather strap."

Andrew Pilgrim shared a vivid account of his encounter. He scored seven marks out of forty-nine on a test of seven long division sums, or as a clever student described it, zero out of forty-two. He remembered the "blows": "Each syllable was visited with a firm entreaty which involved the seven-times-table and certain principles of long division."

Sure, there were other methods of disciplining children that would have achieved the same results, but they all stressed that at Merrivale, corporal punishment was administered with "fairness and love." At times, Teacher was angry and sometimes raised her voice; she did not like "talking back," but while students were "chastised, they were never vilified."

Antonio Rowe could not recall one time he got the strap and did not deserve it. He got into some trouble, he admitted. "It ensured discipline and order and that there were consequences for bad behaviour." He lamented that in the present time only two extremes are seen—brutality or no disciplinary action at all. He thought that the strap was applied successfully as was evident from "the limitless love" Merrivale students have for Teacher.

*

With new insights on disciplining children, alternative strategies were eventually implemented; the removal of a privilege, like ringing the school bell, a shortened lunch break, or a ban from the play area, which some students saw as torture. A child could be subjected to a timeout and be seated right next to his or her teacher or, worse yet, sit right next to Teacher with the threatening strap lurking as a reminder. Non-verbal communication was also effective; a stern look was often enough to convey displeasure.

But even with these initiatives, Avis Carrington expressed her belief that "spanking has its place." The withdrawal of the child was an extreme consequence reserved for those who failed to comply with the principles of the school. However, in its fifty-one-year history, no child was ever expelled.

The UN intervention was too late to save one student. For Ian, the journey to and from school was a hop and a skip across from his bedroom. Little wonder he often forgot where home ended, and school began.

"She was harsher with me than others," he recalls. "I was a reflection of her. In an attempt to avoid bias she went in the opposite direction. I got a pretty tough deal sometimes." But his mother the teacher got the last word. "Those who broke the rules got a spanking. Ian broke more rules than others," she explained.

After consulting with his classmates Ian found out that he made some errors and sneaked into his mother's room and changed the answers on a test. He knew the books had not been marked, but was not aware they had been checked. This time the strap was administered behind closed doors, but the sheepish grin on his face as he emerged from the bedroom told the tale of his encounter with the strap. On other occasions, the whole class witnessed the consequence of being "hard-ears."

Ian believes, sometimes strongly, that parents should never teach their own children; should this view also apply to grandparents and their grandchildren? If Gran was disappointed that her grandchildren did not attend Merrivale, she was discreet in her response. Merrivale was a special institution of learning, a happy place to school a child, and Avis Carrington was a teacher par excellence; but there were other considerations. For Phillipa, Julian's mother, it was the matter of favouritism.

"I think immediately it was so that he [Julian] was neither given preferential treatment nor that he would have the pressure of being Avis' grandson and perhaps just not being himself. Also, it made it special for him to go visit and stay over. It was a great place to go and not be associated with school," she said. "I don't think it was Avis who may have given preferential treatment, but it could have been awkward for the other teaching staff."

The choice made to school the grandchildren elsewhere did not go unnoticed by their grandmother. She thought it was the best idea. "It is easy to compare children especially when they are family members, and this may have caused tension," she shared when reflecting on the decision; and was quick to concede that Ian was held to a higher standard than the other students. He memorialised the leather strap in a dialect poem written to commemorate the thirtieth anniversary of the school:

> Dat strap share nuff, nuff, nuff blows
> From 1959 till now
> I feel dat de leather dat da mek from
> Come off a real strong cow.

What was not revealed in the poem was his tendency to lead his classmates astray. His mother the teacher may have been conscious of being partial to her son and opted to be tougher. Yet, he was quick to acknowledge how he and others benefitted from their education at Merrivale.

> But you know when you look back over the years
> Yuh really have to say
> De edication de strap and everything
> mek we wuh we is today...

> But now that we get big
> And nobody can call any uh we a fool
> We can hold we head high and be real proud
> Dat we went to Merrivale School

The success of the school did not go unnoticed. The Order of Barbados is a system of four levels of awards given for high meritorious service or achievement in science, the arts, literature, sports, civic duties, or any endeavour worthy of national recognition. Avis Carrington was awarded the Silver Crown of Merit in the Barbados Independence Awards of 1994. In 2018 she would receive the highest national award, the Dame of St Andrew.

Avisene (Avis) Carrington and her sister Constance Inniss were featured with eighty-nine other outstanding principals, compiled by historian Dr Henderson Carter, in *Shaping a Nation: Principals of Barbadian Schools 1900-1980*. The project, which was the brainchild of then Prime Minister Owen Arthur, was intended as a "humble tribute" to Barbadian primary and secondary school head teachers of the twentieth century who, through their service, "built a nation." Also honoured in this tribute were Ignatius Byer, Irving Wilson and the renowned Charles Wilkinson "Wilkie" Cumberbatch, all colleagues of Avis at St Giles' Boys' School.

NINE

"A family in harmony will strive in everything." —Chinese proverb

The Rao family meeting with the Carringtons. Merrivale student Mrudulah Rao, shown here in a red blouse, lived with the Carringtons when her family moved to Dominica.

Home-School-Family

AVIS Carrington had achieved her objective. For students, parents and staff, Merrivale was one big happy family. When she invited children into her home, she merged two powerful agents of socialisation. The home, a child's first classroom is the place where children are taught norms and values and provided with safety, comfort and love. At school, children acquire knowledge and social skills which prepare them to live with other members of the society. The Carrington home and Merrivale School became an extended home-school-family built on a solid foundation of love, generosity and support.

Mrs Carrington and the teaching staff were like mothers, Mr Carrington was the father figure, and Gran was in the background until the late seventies. The parents of classmates were affectionately called "Auntie" or "Uncle." Ms Ruby Applewhaite, housekeeper and cook, and Ms Marielot Coppin, caretaker, were part of the extended family. Mr Grazette, the gardener, and Mr Murray, the handyman, worked at the school until their retirement in the late seventies, and were replaced by the younger Mark Graham, a longstanding family member. Mr Leslie Murray, the contractor, not to be confused with Murray the handyman, and Mr Francis, the joiner, offered occasional but long-term services, earning themselves family status.

The construction of the school building did not end the use of the house, which was never out of bounds. With a polite, "Excuse me, Teacher," children moved about freely, whether planning events or constructing large projects, or when practising for the end-of-term concert. It was the venue for staff meetings and sessions with parents, a sick bay for children, a refuge for the occasional child left at school; and it provided the safety and comfort for those students who needed special moments with Teacher.

*

Avis Carrington did not only open her home to students, she followed in the footsteps of her mother and became an adoptive mum. Albert and Rita Maxwell, who lived in Brooklyn, New York, were close friends of Vere and Avis and spent vacations at each other's homes. The Maxwells moved back to Barbados in 1973 and spent a few months at "Shenstone" before moving to their home in St Joseph. Albert took ill and passed away, leaving Rita to raise their only child Melvin. When Rita developed health problems and her condition worsened, she made only one heartfelt request of the Carringtons. She died peacefully knowing that they would provide Melvin with the warmth and safety that comes with a loving home.

The transition for Melvin was easy. The Carrington children were like the brothers and sister he never had; especially Ian, who was closer in age and interests. They spent days roaming the property, riding bikes, and racing Melvin's favourite Scalextric toy cars on a fifteen-foot circuit set up in the schoolhouse. The track, model cars and accessories were stored during the school term; the "race-car drivers" could hardly wait until the next vacation or long weekend to "rev up the engines."

"Teacher cared about every student and wanted them to do well," recalls Melvin. This was in sharp contrast to what he experienced at his Brooklyn School. He graduated from Alleyne School, a grammar school in St Andrew and had no thoughts or desire to return to the United States; but his new family felt that, at age eighteen, he should return to his country of birth to attend college and benefit fully from his citizenship. He knew that his adoptive parents always had his best interests at heart and trusted their judgment, but 28 November, 1978, the day he left Barbados is forever "etched" in his mind. He went to live with his godfather and missed the warmth and protection he had come to cherish. The Carringtons were never far away. He visited his family home, especially at Christmas and Uncle Vere was in constant contact as he managed his legal matters in Barbados. Although challenging at first, the move back to the United States made Melvin a man.

There was another "adoption," this one for a shorter time. Ten-year old Mrudula was a Class Three student when her father accepted a job in Dominica. Her parents feared that the move would interrupt her primary education and opted instead to leave their daughter with the Carringtons. The Rao family was not surprised when Mrs Carrington accepted. She was warm and compassionate and known to shed tears with students over their 11-plus results. Mrudula spent a full year at "Shenstone"; decades later, she is still thought of as a little sister.

The Carrington household and its extended family did not only compensate for her parents' absence but caused Mrudula to reminisce on the relationship she had with the relatives she left behind in India; she had been especially close to her grandmother. Mrudula went on to be a Board-Certified Psychiatrist and an Adjunct Professor, Department of Psychiatry, at the University of Texas Health Science Centre in San Antonio, where she lives with her husband and three children.

Late in 2012, Mrudula made a surprise call; she was coming home for the holidays. She walked through each room and perused snap-shots that captured the warm memories of her home and school life.

The lively playground, the spaces where groups of children assembled with their teachers, full of enthusiasm and eager to learn were now vacant. Mrudula was not prepared for the silence. Only thoughts of the special bond she shared with Teacher would bring back the warmth and life of her experience at "Shenstone."

"She holds a very special place in my heart as she strived hard to meet my needs, as a ten-year-old girl, in my parents' and siblings' absence. She has a warm and pure heart. She is an exquisite lady! To this day I have yet to meet a person as compassionate and gentle as Mrs Carrington."

*

Avis balanced the roles of wife, mother, teacher, and leader with an abundance of help that never went unacknowledged in this extended family. Some roles were clearly defined, but family members also pitched in when needed. Avis' mother was sometimes the chief cook, trainer of the household staff, or assistant to the babysitter. When Vere was in London to complete his studies and Avis was a resident student at Erdiston Teachers' Training College, Gran moved to the Pine Road residence to take care of the children.

The nieces and nephews in the family were always available to assist Aunt Dan; she celebrated her one hundred and third birthday on 29 May, 2019. Pat and Hazel took turns living with her at Martindale's Road when she was headmistress at St Michael's Girls' School, until Ronnie moved in with her permanently. Shelley would become her principal caregiver, with assistance from Averil and Hazel.

A much too punctual Granddad chauffeured the grandchildren from primary school to Pine Road. He arrived so early they lamented the loss of playtime, but soon made friends at Merrivale. Avis' car was always made available to Ian and Hazel when they were home on vacation. And Shelley knew the secret to being a popular aunt when she loaned her brand-new car to her nieces to go to the beach. She also took on the role of French tutor when she coached her niece Ria for the Caribbean Examinations Council (CXC) exam.

Avis is especially thankful for all the help with the day-to-day running of the school; but she is particularly mindful that her husband Vere was her anchor and main support. His contribution was that of administrator which allowed her to focus primarily on instruction and leadership. Gran, who had aspirations of becoming a teacher, also made her contribution, albeit from a safe distance. A window at the back of the house offered her a wide-angled view of the school, and she knew every child by name. Good behaviour was maintained with a purposed glance and head held at just the right angle. Pursed lips conveyed disapproval, while a warm smile, accompanied by a nod of the head, reinforced good behaviour.

As part of their chores, the Carrington siblings transformed the dining room into a classroom. On a typical Friday afternoon, it was restored to some semblance of a home when a line of students with chairs held high over their heads wended their way to the storeroom located behind the garage and packed away the school furniture. Shelley and Ian made the ice blocks—a frozen mixture of milk, sugar, water, and food dye wrapped in foil; these would become legendary. And every December, they wrapped the Christmas gifts, one for each child. With age came greater responsibility; Ian supervised the gate and ensured the safe delivery of children to their parents and Shelley assisted with the clerical work. While she received a small stipend, Ian continued to complain that he was "paid not one cent for these long and arduous days of work."

Ronnie had long moved away from home, but Shelley and Ian continued to help, and both tested their skills in the classroom. Shelley had no interest in making teaching her career, but her efforts were commendable. However, her younger brother failed to make the grade.

When Ian attempted his first teaching assignment, he was a student at Barbados Community College. After years of watching his mother, he felt qualified and was determined to impress her; she would have been pleased if at least one of the children had shown interest in the teaching profession.

His strategy was to assert his authority immediately, but the Merrivale students could spot a novice from a mile away.

"Sir, can I go to the bathroom?" one little boy asked politely.

"No," the trainee replied firmly.

"But please, sir," the now impatient boy pleaded.

"No," he reiterated, failing to grasp the urgency of the request. "You only just came in." With that the boy rose and moved briskly past the teacher to the washroom.

"You all right," he grumbled on his way out. "You up there cooling out."

This left no doubt in Ian's mind that teaching was not his calling. He was content to limit his responsibilities at Merrivale to decorating the school for special events. After moving away from home, he and his family of helpers returned at Christmas to deck the halls of the home and the school with shiny streamers and strings of twinkling lights.

Parents were exceptional, either as volunteers or as part of the elected PTA. In a joint project with past students, the roof of the garage, which housed the library and an open teaching space, was replaced. They gave generously of their time, money and other resources to see the project to completion. Avis was reluctant at first to accept any assistance, especially with maintenance to the property. The school was still, after all, her home. She was profoundly grateful for the contribution to the school, and accepted on condition that the PTA manage all financial transactions.

The ancillary staff maintained the physical spaces and contributed to the overall climate of the workplace. Like the teachers and students, they saw Merrivale as their family. Applewhaite was employed as house-keeper in 1966 and was there until the school closed its doors in 2010. Her first day on the job, she was met by a bright-eyed Ian, ten years old at the time, who gave her a tour of the home and school. Past students recalled her fondly as one of the constants, not only for them but she was there when their children became students.

Applewhaite was informed of the family's love of rice but was free to prepare what she saw fit. At twelve o'clock every weekday for forty-four years, she served a hot meal to Mrs Carrington who sat in the same chair at the eastern end of the dining table, often hurrying her lunch to spend time with a child in need. As the school grew, the management of a small canteen that operated from the kitchen was added to Applewhaite's responsibilities.

Hot dogs, "the best ever," and hamburgers were the main items on the menu. The signature treat, the milky ice blocks, were replaced with frozen Kool-Aid until the arrival of the "suck-a-bubby." The frozen ice came in a variety of colours and flavours and was eaten through a small hole bitten into one of the corners of the plastic bag that held the icy treat.

*

Avis described Marielot Coppin as a "gem" of the ancillary staff. She was employed in the early seventies and worked until failing eyesight forced her to retire in 1998; she was eighty years old. Twice a day, she walked from Hart's Gap to Pine Road, and she did not leave until every nook of the school was clean and tidy. She often stayed beyond her stipulated hours knowing that Vere would give her a ride home. When an ailing sister in the United States called on Ms Coppin, she took a year off to attend to her sibling; however, she made it abundantly clear that she was returning to her job, and that was exactly what she did. When Coppin's eyes failed and she was no longer able to take care of herself, the Carringtons facilitated her move to the Geriatric Hospital. Over the years she received several visits from the family and enjoyed reminiscing about the good old days at Merrivale. On 17 July, 2018, Governor General Dame Sandra Mason toasted Coppin who "always knew" that she would live to see her hundredth birthday. Erene Howell from St John became the new caretaker. She came with a recommendation from Applewhaite and fitted right in. She spent three years on the job before the school closed its doors.

Mark the groundsman first came to Merrivale as an eleven-year-old when he visited the school with his mother, who was filling in for Ms Coppin. When he came of age, Mark was asked to help out in the yard and was employed in 1978. Even when the school closed, he continued to serve as gardener and handyman. His tasks ranged from painting to car washing and odd jobs like changing light bulbs in the home. Mark admired Mr Carrington, whom he described as a "perfect gentleman," but was particularly devoted to Mrs Carrington. "I would do anything for Mrs Carrington. If I live to be one hundred and she need me, I would be there for her."

Mrs Carrington lost contact with Rawle Francis the joiner after the school closed, but constantly wondered about his welfare. The "chair-man," as he was affectionately called took over from the elderly Mr Mann and maintained the furniture at Merrivale. He lit up the school with his cheerful personality, jolly laugh and promise of new furniture. The chance meeting at the Annual Flower Show 2017, at Ball's Plantation was a mix of warmth, joy and tears.

For over thirty years, Francis as he was called, built and repaired the chairs with seats made of woven fibre rush, a twisted paper used for that purpose. "Write my name on that one," a child once requested, hoping a refurbished chair would come his way.

"There was always happiness at that school," Francis recalled. "We would talk. She wanted to know how life is and asked about the family.

She kept food on my table. Many days I went to that school with no money in my pocket, and I would tell her, 'I come, I hungry, I have nothing at all.' And I would leave there with a cheque in my hand, sometimes for two hundred dollars, whether I find chairs to repair or not. I would drink a 'grog' and use the rest to put food pun my table."

Avis was all charm and grace, trying to change the subject, deflecting the praise, trying to shut him up. Then he shared the reason for the mixed emotions. Only four weeks had passed since the death of his wife and he was in deep mourning. After expressions of sympathy, the conversation switched again to Merrivale. Immediately his smile broadened, and the tears gave way to a twinkle in his eyes. "She is a nice lady; hear what I tell you? A real nice lady."

Avis met Shirley James in May 1992 when she became the traffic warden at the pedestrian crossing on Pine Road, used almost exclusively by Merrivale school. Like most visitors to the school, she found the children "mannerly and friendly," and soon developed a close bond which extended to the parents and teachers. The relationship shifted to business when she sought permission from Mr Carrington to become the resident snack lady. This meant that Mrs Carrington could monitor what was sold to the children.

Prior to this arrangement, candy, bubble gum and Chiclets, a peppermint flavoured gum, had a way of turning up at the school without explanation. This was a clandestine business that operated without Mrs Carrington's approval. Even though the practice was discouraged, the banned items would reappear. Not everyone was allowed entry to the candy ring. A student detective happened upon the operation; rather than snitch on the perpetrators, he was sworn to secrecy and managed to gain membership.

Shirley enjoyed her new association with the school. Her tray was stacked with Skittles, Cheezies, bonbons, corn curls, tamarind balls with pepper, Cry Baby, sour bubble gum and Jolly Rancher hard candies, all in an eye-catching and mouth-watering display. The young mother was grateful for the opportunity to supplement her small income. She was also a fixture at end-of-term and birthday parties and was a guest at graduation ceremonies.

The relationship became occasionally strained when Shirley expanded the business to include fishcakes and chicken wings and she found herself in competition with the PTA and canteen for the limited sales. Some thought Shirley should curtail this activity, especially when the school was raising funds. Mrs Carrington was torn; while she understood the argument, she could not deny the snack lady the opportunity to earn a few extra dollars.

Mrs Carrington's generosity was also extended to parents. She purchased textbooks and other supplies in bulk from Cloister Bookstore and sold them at cost, a gesture intended to save parents time and money. During times of hardship that impacted the payment of fees, she was reluctant to confront parents and did so only when pressured by the school's management. Payment plans were negotiated to ease parents, even when it meant using her savings to make up the shortfall. When a couple shared their decision to transfer two siblings to public school, they were allowed to continue for the cost of one child. The girls were very good students, and she feared that the move might have affected their progress.

Merrivale was not just a school, it was a family home and a haven, and sometimes Teacher found herself in the role of babysitter long after the school day had ended. No child wanted to be left at school after hours, and certainly not after sundown. An invitation to join Teacher indoors did little to ease the discomfort, which bordered on embarrassment. Homework was done, snacks were served, and a little television was allowed. Teacher's biggest concern was how to reach parents to assure them that their child was comfortable and safe.

"When the call from my parents eventually came, I remember her on the phone being so understanding and reassuring that I was okay, that I took it upon myself when we got home, to quarrel with both my parents and be enraged on her behalf, because I felt that she had been just too nice to do it herself."

Some children arrived at school before Teacher could change into her garden clothes. There was no prior notice, on the Monday morning that Jill was dropped off exceptionally early; her father had to be at the office before seven. If Teacher was annoyed, she hid it well, because Jill saw no sign of irritation. After an apology for her floral housecoat and head tie, she made a hasty change to dungarees and a cotton knit shirt. On the following day when the doorbell rang, she was appropriately dressed and ready to receive the child, who followed her around while she tended the garden.

The home-school-family developed a mutually beneficial relationship with the Girls' Industrial Union (GIU) which offers a variety of classes to participants. The union is situated on the lot to the south of the school which was a field of sugarcane when the Carringtons moved to Pine Road. The elegant building sat at the back of the property, leaving room for a large car park at the front of the lot. This was used by Merrivale parents for drop-offs and pickups; in return, the GIU received an annual donation from the school.

In a show of community spirit, Avis reached out to The Almair Home for assisted living situated at the corner of Pine Road and 4th Avenue Belleville. Every Christmas, the Class 5 students entertained the residents.

This was Merrivale at its very best. The school had exceeded what Avis Carrington had dreamed of for the small playgroup. The home-school-family was a place of love, a place of caring and sharing, kindness and compassion; a place of community. These attributes provided an anchor that kept the family grounded in times of challenge.

TEN

"The more you praise and celebrate your life, the more there is in life to celebrate." —Oprah Winfrey

Simply Teacher: The Life of Avis Carrington

In 1994, the Christmas family gathering hosted by Pat Byer, Avis' niece and first hired teacher at Merrivale (second from left). Avis is first from left.

Challenge-Triumph-Celebration

LIKE most families, the Carringtons endured everyday life with its exhilarating highs, mundane lows, and the pain that comes with loss. When life was challenging, another activity was always just around the corner to bring back a sense of normalcy; a new school year with the joy and laughter of the children, the school fair, graduation, a birthday, Easter, Mother's Day, Christmas. These traditions developed over time and merged seamlessly from home to school to family.

Avis has endured her share of pain and loss; at 102, she has outlived school-family members, relatives and close friends. She could not remember the year, but her father died before she was married in 1947; and her mother, with whom she shared a very close relationship, passed away in 1978. When Vere died in August 1993, he and Avis had been married for forty-six years. She said goodbye to the mother and son pair of Rita and Kenneth Pile, friends who lived on 3rd Avenue Belleville and were constants at the annual Christmas luncheon. May, who was one of the children that the Innisses took in, passed away in 2018.

It was not the Byer's turn to host; Yet Arthur Byer, acting on a premonition, or so it seemed, requested that the luncheon be held at his St George home. He passed away in August 1985.

The family lost Erdine to Alzheimer's; the disease, which results in memory loss and withdrawal, robbed the family of Erdine's warmth and charm before she passed away in 2007. Avis cherished the close friendship she enjoyed with her sister and has missed her dearly. The death of Erdine's eldest daughter Pat in 2016 was sad for everyone, but especially Avis. She was the first grandchild in the Inniss household, and the first hired teacher at Merrivale.

Vere's decline was gradual and went almost unnoticed by parents, teachers and students as he continued to meet the responsibilities of head of household and chief steward of Merrivale. Every evening, he made sure that the school building was secured, and the gate was locked before retiring for the evening. So many were inspired by his caring nature and dedication to the school, especially his wife Avis. "Vere was one of the nicest persons I ever met," she said. "A very special person." On the 30th anniversary of the school held at Sam Lord's Castle in St Philip, Vere strode across the floor to the Bette Midler song "Wind Beneath My Wings." It was a fitting tribute.

> Did you ever know that you're my hero?[...]
> I can fly higher than an eagle
> For you are the wind beneath my wings.

After Vere's death, Avis focused on maintaining the integrity of the school. She added the role of administrator to her duties and rallied with help from family members.

Marcelle Best, a certified accountant and family friend, was asked to assist with the financial operations. Her role was to analyse income and expenses to derive the tax liabilities, and to file the relevant taxes. Avis insisted on paying Marcelle a stipend despite her resistance. After two years, she had acquired the necessary accounting skills and assumed responsibility for these tasks.

In 1995 the family faced yet another challenge. Ian was studying for his master's degree at the University of Exeter in the UK, when he was diagnosed with a malignant tumour of the adrenal gland. The family would see him endure seven hours of surgery, suffer excruciating pain, extreme weight loss and a long and slow recuperation. Mum was distressed, suffered a loss of appetite and spent many sleepless nights. Ian developed an additional problem when stress on his deltoid muscle during surgery resulted in the paralysis of his right arm. The initial diagnosis was hard, and Mum was so distraught that it was thought better to spare her an additional worry. She was devastated when she learned of Ian's condition, but the arm responded well to therapy, and he made a full recovery. He returned to the UK to complete his studies and continued in good health.

The sudden death of Stephen Alleyne in October 2007 left his former teacher in a state of grief. Avis remembered him as academically outstanding and one of the nicest students she ever taught. He excelled at primary school and attended Harrison College and was the first male student from Merrivale to win the Barbados Scholarship. His appointment as CEO of Life of Barbados (now Sagicor) also made him the first Barbadian actuary to head an insurance firm in the island. Stephen also served as one of the directors of the West Indies Cricket Board. Locally, he was the President of the Barbados Cricket Association and was the chief executive of the Barbados Local Organising Committee for Cricket World Cup 2007.

Avis expressed a genuine interest in the home-school-family members, enquiring about relatives, especially when they were ill. She allowed teachers time to tend to elderly parents and was present at the funerals of school-family members. Avis felt that she should be present to offer support. One student was so moved when she saw Teacher at her mother's funeral, she remarked, "It makes me love her even more." Avis was not well on that day but insisted on being present to support the family, even if it meant leaving before the end of the service.

Avis was not one to dwell in a fog of despair; even in times of sadness, she would reflect on her life and be grateful for her blessings. She and Vere raised three children, each successful in his or her chosen field. Ronnie is a noted photographer and videographer. He is CEO of Carrington Photo-Creations and Corporate Imaging, two companies that produce visual communications materials. Among his other projects are his Overseas Photographic Adventure Tours, Photo Adventure Workshops and the highly successful Photographic Tour of Barbados. The last is a mix of photo tips and techniques presented together with information about the island and its culture. Ronnie has been conducting photo tours for the cruise industry for over twenty years and has won the Princess Cruise Line Award of Excellence for over ten consecutive years. He has served on the boards of the Caribbean Broadcasting Corporation and the National Cultural Foundation.

Shelley followed in her dad's footsteps and became a career civil servant. Her first assignment was Research Assistant in the Bureau of Women's Affairs, now the Bureau of Gender Affairs, before being promoted to Administrative Officer and later Senior Administrative Officer. She served in several ministries before her appointment to the post of Deputy Permanent Secretary and was assigned to the Ministry of Labour. She was promoted to Permanent Secretary in 2011 and served in that capacity in the Ministry of Tourism. Shelley retired from the government service in December 2014, and offered corporate secretarial consultancy services and human resource development services to government and private agencies.

*

The change from home-school to public secondary school got off to a great start for Merrivale's first pupil. He was well grounded in the principles of mathematics and grammar and was a well-rounded student. But outside of the watchful eye of his mother the teacher, Ian found himself once again at the receiving end of the rod of correction. His grades slipped and he repeated a year level which landed him in Form 2^4, strategically situated near the gate. Another failure could lead to expulsion. A pep-talk from Canon Ivor Jones, a noted educator who had a passion for teaching, renewed his interest in his studies.

After stints in the government service and the Barbados Development Bank, Ian rose to the level of Director of Bank Supervision, Central Bank of Barbados. In 2000, he was appointed to the post of Financial Expert with the UN Global Programme against Money Laundering in the UN Office of Drugs and Crime (UNDC) in Vienna. Two years later he joined the staff of the International Monetary Fund as a Senior Financial Sector Expert. He provides technical assistance to central banks in diverse places ranging from Europe to East Africa and Asia. He also served for four years as a Bank Supervision Advisor, East AFRITAC (The Regional Technical Assistance Centre) headquartered at the Central Bank of Tanzania in Dar es Salaam.

Avis was proud of the outstanding alumni, and kept a record of their academic success neatly inscribed in a special book. Sixteen past students were awarded the Barbados Scholarship and nine received the Barbados Exhibition. Also noted were those who have risen to prominence in Barbados through their public service. The Honourable Mia Amor Mottley, QC, MP had served as Minister of Education, Attorney-General, and Leader of the Opposition. She was sworn in as Barbados' first female Prime Minister on 25 May, 2018.

Other alumni are Donna Babb-Agard, QC, first female Director of Public Prosecutions; Averil Byer, former Senior Vice President of Marketing of the Barbados Tourism Authority, and the founder and CEO of Aplomb, a marketing consultancy firm; Alissandra Cummins,

Director of the Barbados Museum & Historical Society and Barbados' representative on the Executive Board of UNESCO; Dr William Duguid, an implantologist, oral surgeon, and Minister of Transport Works and Maintenance in the 2018 cabinet; Yolande Forde, Barbados' first female criminologist and former Director of the National Task Force on Crime Prevention; Philip Nicholls, attorney-at-law, former Secretary of the Barbados Cricket Association, and former President of the Pickwick Cricket Club; Brenda Pope, former Advisory Partner, KPMG; Andrew Sealy, former sports journalist with the Caribbean Broadcasting Corporation and former Executive Secretary of the West Indies Cricket Board; Richard Sealy, a former Minister of Tourism.

Dr Marcia Burrowes was the Coordinator and Lecturer in Cultural Studies at the University of the West Indies, Cave Hill; and Andrew Pilgrim, QC, was a criminal defence lawyer and former President of the Barbados Bar Association. Apart from their primary roles, they were well-known in the performing arts. And in the field of music and arts there were Nicholas Brancker, a Grammy-nominated, classically trained musician and producer; Arturo Tappin, the jazz-fusion saxophonist; and Earthworks' David Spieler, a noted ceramist and businessman.

Avis was proudest of those students who attained their goals despite their challenging circumstances; her face would light up with enthusiasm when sharing the accomplishments of these exceptional students: the child who had to be coached daily and went on to excel at secondary school; the dyslexic boy who could not read at age eight but gained entry to secondary school, completed tertiary education and was appointed to a post in the civil service; the seven-year-old who was transferred from a leading private school because he was not "making progress," and became a doctor of psychiatry; the child who struggled with reading but gave the vote of thanks at his graduation.

It seems as if Avis was gifted with the patience and the compassion to teach children who needed extra tuition, and often regretted that training in remedial education was not available early in her career.

*

One other event that brought Avis an abundance of joy and satisfaction was the arrival of grandchildren. She was stern, that's how she saw herself, and agonised about how they would relate to her, and she to them. The answer came soon enough. The doting grandparents were overjoyed when Julian arrived in December of 1982 to Ronnie and Phillipa, and the apprehension disappeared. Julian soon showed a preference for his more placid and patient Granddad, who delighted in reading him a bedtime story when he overnighted at "Shenstone." A jealous Gran offered, but Julian showed no interest until the night that Vere was unavailable, and Avis used her teaching skills to "moo," "cluck," "oink" and "meow" her way into his heart.

Ian and his wife Hazel added two granddaughters to the family. Ria was born in 1984 and she became a big sister to Kori three years later. The due date for the second child was a mere ten days away. As a precaution, days were spent with the in-laws. The year was 1987, the last day of March, and the school was on Easter break. The day spent at Pine Road went by quickly; after chatting, watching TV, a light lunch, browsing through a few magazines, and a brief nap, it was pick-up time. As Avis said her goodbyes, she cautioned with pointed finger and a wry smile.

"You know what tomorrow is?" she said, trying but failing to hide the jest in her warning. "Don't go and do anything foolish."

Kori was born before daybreak on the following morning. On his way back from the Queen Elizabeth Hospital, the beaming father stopped at the family home in Pine Road to share the good news with his mother.

"You think you can fool me?" she said. "I know that today is All

149

Fools' Day." It took a lot of persuasion to convince Avis that her daughter-in-law had birthed her third grandchild on the first day of April.

Avis wasted no time wondering what her grandchildren would call her. The Carrington siblings called their maternal grandmother "Gran"; maybe she wanted to continue in that tradition. However, that was not the reason given for this one request.

"I am not to be called Granny," she stated emphatically. "A granny is an old, old person. Just call me 'Gran.'" As it turned out, that title was already taken by the maternal grandmother. "Granny" was eight years younger and had become a grandmother seven years earlier than Avis.

Distance was not an issue when Avis wanted to see her grandchildren. She visited Ian when he moved the family to Vienna, Austria, in 2000, and again in Falls Church, Virginia, when he joined the IMF. In the summer of 2004, Avis paid a second visit to Virginia. This time a road trip to Toronto to visit colleges and some sightseeing was included. This was Ian's first adventure driving that far north and the ten-hour trip turned into twelve hours of a "never again" gruelling drive. What made it worth the long hours was a visit to see her grandson Julian who had moved there with his mother. Gran visited Julian again in June 2017; she was three months shy of her ninety-ninth birthday. She first attended the wedding of a former student in Michigan and took advantage of the proximity to see him.

Growing up 2,400 miles away from Barbados and pre-Skype, Julian has some regrets about the little time he spent getting to know his grandmother. Julian recalled vividly how she would drive to the then Big B supermarket in Worthing to indulge his late-evening grape craving when none of the juicy fruits were to be found in the fridge at Pine Road.

"Neither that distance, though, nor the relative infrequency of our visits together has diminished the impression she's made on me. Gran's kindness is the stuff of my earliest memories."

Avis was unfailingly generous to her grandson, but it was her grace, serenity and absolute decency that have resonated most strongly with him. Teacher though she was, Gran guided him less by exacting lesson than by effortless example. His British grandmother in contrast offered him strict elocution instructions befitting the young gentleman she wanted him to become. Julian imagined that she was no different with her Merrivale students.

"They, like me, will have benefitted most of all simply from the opportunity to know her," said Julian, "and to emulate the dignity and poise that she still very much possesses, even as her century approaches."

Her granddaughter Ria captured her admiration of her Gran in a youthful poem of childhood remembrance:

> She is
> Smiling brown eyes.
> Gentle scoldings and warm hugs
> Piles of sparkling beads and bangles
> And sweeping kaleidoscope skirts to hide behind.
> She is Saturday morning supermarket trips
> that always ended with Archie comics and candy bars.
> And weekend sleepovers curled up on the couch
> with toasted cheese paste sandwiches
> and half-frozen Coca-Cola right out the glass bottle.
> She is as radiant and as vibrant now as she was then.
> Your Mrs Carrington,
> She is just Gran to me.

For Kori, it was Gran's love, tender care and kindness that stood out. Years later, she was still in awe of the oversized gift bags laden with treasure from the annual Miami Christmas-shopping sprees:

books, candy, clothing, games, toys! It was always the best present the grandchildren received. But what Kori admired most was her grandmother's dedication to teaching and the love she had for the students who passed through Merrivale.

"There is no doubt," Kori said, "that teaching and nurturing students are her passion. She always has vivid memories and stories of her students, and her face lights up when they come to visit. She has made an impact on their lives as well as mine."

The generation gap may threaten the relationship between grandparents and their grandchildren, not so with Avis and her grands; they have their own social lives, but the bonds they established in their childhood have kept them close, even as her circle has diminished over the years. She is transported to a place of glee when the grandchildren visit, especially when the family gathered to give thanks for blessings, and adversity was forgotten. Her triumph over misfortune belied a major issue that was looming; but first the home-school family would celebrate Christmas.

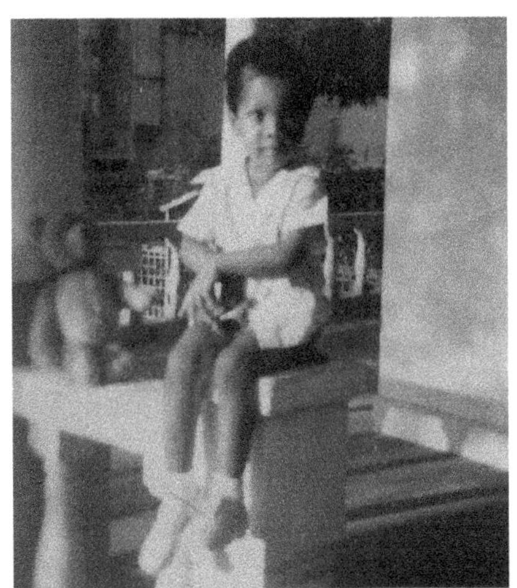

School life.

Top: Avis' younger son Ian for whom the Merrivale Playgroup was founded.

Above: Avis Carrington and the graduating class of 1967.

Top: Ronnie in the midst of the overgrown bush on the rise at the back of the family home before it was landscaped and became a playground "with character."

Above: The eastern side of the property was cleared and landscaped. The school building is in the foreground, nestled in the shadow of trees and tropical shrubs. The family home is in the background. (Photo courtesy Michelle Marshall, Altman Real Estate.)

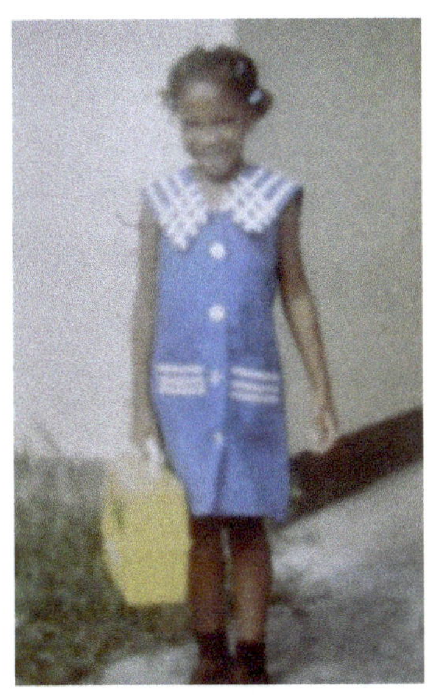

Top: Kimberly Sandiford, class of 1993, wearing the junior uniform. Top right: Senior uniform; Yolande Forde, class of 1976.

Below: Students purchasing treats from Shirley the vendor, who was also the crossing guard.

Opposite top: The dance troupe at Merrivale. Opposite bottom: End-of-term dance recital.

Above: The annual athletic meet where everyone received a trophy for participation.

Top: The reception class. Field trips were planned for students of all ages.

Teacher is surrounded by the graduation class of 1993.

CHOOL GRADUATION   CLASS OF 1993
SOM   DONE

ELEVEN

"Christmas is the season of joy, of holiday greetings exchanged, of gift-giving, and families united." —Norman Vincent Peale

Christmas at Merrivale (circa early Sixties).

A Very Merry Christmas

THERE is nothing that Avis Carrington enjoys more than Christmas; "it's the most invigorating time" of her life. "What do you want for Christmas" is the question from her childhood that sparked the excitement that lasted into her adulthood. Avis, following the lead of her sister Erdine, would always choose a doll, while Dan the studious one would choose a book.

Grandmother Mary Wiltshire arrived by train from St Andrew, warm and sweet and full of Christmas joy. All eyes were on the woven basket which failed to contain the aroma of baked goodies packed inside. Avis could not wait to bite into her favourite, the cassava pone; for soon her grandmother's treats and Mama Inniss' cakes and sorrel would be shared with the neighbours, all in the spirit of the season.

The Christmas luncheon emerged as a family tradition that alternated between the Inniss (Aunt Dan), Byer and Carrington households. What Avis loved most about the gathering, was the warmth of the whole family in one place, and the occasional surprise visit from friends, especially those from abroad. May, who had lived with the Innisses as a child, travelled home every year from New York.

The airport was always abuzz with families meeting and greeting each other. A glimpse of relatives as they disembarked would set off a frenzied mass of waves and shouting, as if the visitors would not soon emerge from the arrival hall. Eager eyes scanned swollen suitcases, wondering what holiday treasure was buried inside; all adding to the joyfulness of the season.

For the school family, it was the annual end-of-term Christmas party and concert. The Christmas season started early at Merrivale. It's mid-December, and the strings of coloured lights around the home and the school signal the countdown to the last day of the term, "It's party day", "The best day ever." Students trade their uniformed look for trendy T-shirts, jeans and sneakers with bold patterns of their favourite cartoon characters. Some girls wear their Sunday best with tall white stockings, and some decorate their hair with an array of colourful bobbles and bows.

The highlight of the day was Teacher's arrival. The long driveway was her catwalk, as she delicately strutted in her well-coordinated outfits. The students often greeted her with whistles, cheers of approval, and a standing ovation. Avis had vivid recollections of her mother's stylish clothing, and how it transformed her from a housewife, who was stripped of her profession, to a woman who dared to stand tall in her elegance. This must have influenced her sense of style.

On weekdays, her preference was a pair of slacks and a cotton shirt, which fitted in well with the cool outdoor classroom. But on special occasions?

"She was always dressed to the nines," recalled one student; and said another, "She always looked super glamorous in her slim-fitting pants and gold or silver high-heeled shoes."

Avis never conformed to the notion of dressing to suit one's age; not if it meant that with one's senior years one had to be dull and dowdy. Her appearance was always youthful; in the company of her husband, she was often thought to be his daughter, and in the company of her son

Ronnie, she was often thought to be his wife. Avis fancied accessories; an assortment of necklaces, sets of colourful bangles, a bold handbag, and she was never without a pair of hip sunglasses.

Party day at the end of the Michaelmas term was always extra special. Practice for the Christmas show was held in the house, and the activities were guarded like a "state secret," all adding to the intrigue. Impatient boys explored every possibility of getting a sneak peek at the costumes. They stood on the short wall to the south of the building, climbed the fence, or made up some excuse to get into the house, all to boast about the results of the undercover quest. Shelley had given up on helping her mother with the teaching but was always on hand to assist with practice for the skits, choreography for dances, and on the day of the show she assumed the role of make-up artist.

Brightly coloured streamers and balloons ran the length of the school hall and framed the small stage at the front. The rest of the room had been cleared of furniture except for stacks of chairs arranged to form a balcony at the back of the school hall. This provided senior boys with the best vantage point, using their rank and status to ensure that the well-guarded space was off limits to juniors and girls. Seasonal music streamed from a small boom box mounted at the back of the stage. In the past, a Salsoul Orchestra LP, a long-playing vinyl record, provided a medley of Christmas songs from a record player.

Each class showed off a special talent. It could be a poem, a song, a creative dance or skit; and some brave souls modelled their party clothes. There was singing to popular carols that featured a frosty snowman, reindeer with red noses, and open sleighs on a hot, sunny Caribbean day.

The best part of the party was a toss-up between gorging on the abundance of ice cream, cake and candy, or the gift exchange that included all members of the Merrivale family. Amidst the celebration, the students were reminded of the true meaning of Christmas.

Every year, the Class 5 students entertained the residents of the Almair Home for assisted living. "It's the least you can do for them after deafening them for the school year," Teacher teased, as a reminder to keep down the noise level.

In the fifty-one years of the school, no one could recall a single complaint from the neighbours. They danced and sang and performed comedic skits, shared gifts and served refreshments to the appreciative guests. Even those who were shy at first eventually enjoyed chatting with the old ladies, especially when some of the wheel-chair-bound seniors challenged the students to a race. Their tired eyes lit up and smiles broke through wrinkled faces. Weary bodies swayed ever so gently to the music, and arms, though frail, found the strength to applaud and to hug a child.

It is Avis's turn to host the luncheon, and with the school children gone, the home and garden get her full attention. The transformation started weeks in advance with a run to the hardware store; a paint job, some new patio furniture with matching umbrella, and themed items create a jolly holiday atmosphere. The flower beds were refreshed with a turn of the soil, the lawns mowed, and the hedges trimmed to perfection. Herbaceous flora that flowered quickly were added to bring more colour to the gardens, and any dreary corner was brightened with an assortment of potted plants, in this holiday makeover of her little Eden.

If gardening was Avis' favourite pastime, then seeking out the pleasure that comes from "browsing" was a close second, especially so during the holiday season. The shopping area could be a vegetable or flea market, or a street lined with stores as far as the eye can see; but she was in awe of the enormity of the indoor shopping mall. These facilities housed an array of shops, each unique in its design and festive appeal; creative displays in brightly lit spaces, the smell of new clothes and perfumed places; and for bargain hunters, large red posters that scream BIG SALE to lure the shoppers in.

Every year Avis travelled to Miami with Vere in tow to do her Christmas shopping. She was a dedicated and business-like shopper who covered a lot of ground in a short time and had low tolerance for those who would impede her progress, as one hapless shopping partner discovered. But this was not any shopping partner; this was her daughter-in-law who was invited on a trial basis to accompany the now widowed Avis.

The first day of the trip was spent together, but with her pace slowed, the pair agreed to split up and meet for lunch. By day three, the lunch date was off the table. While Avis was keen to explore the nightlife advertised in bold neon lights, the not-so-brave partner preferred to stay indoors after hours. Not unexpectedly, there were no further invitations to go shopping, except for an occasional visit to a local plant nursery.

*

It was the Saturday before Christmas, and Avis made her way to Cheapside Market in lower Bridgetown. The Fairchild Street Market was a mere five minutes away from home and was the market of choice, until a redevelopment project led to its closure in 2007. Shoppers from all walks of life converged on the continuous rows of chequered stands of bold contrasting shades of colour, which were further enhanced by brightly patterned tablecloths.

Wooden trays overflowed with layers upon layers of fragrant fruits, and aromatic herbs, vegetables and ground provisions. "How you sweet girl" and other pleasantries filled the air as hawkers tried to attract customers. They advertised their produce and haggled over prices, competing against the backdrop of lively Bajan banter, that added to the hustle and bustle of market shopping.

At this time of the year, green peas and sorrel are high on the list and quickly become scarce; but these prized items were always tucked away under the counter for those who had a special relationship with the seller. The market has seen many changes, no doubt some of her favourite vendors have gone, but Avis Carrington remained a constant as she continued her weekly runs to the Bridgetown market.

One last activity remained before the big day. Avis belonged to that group of seniors who have their hair styled, only to cover it with a wig; this was no ordinary wig; it was made of human hair with highlights, always coiffed to perfection and worn with a slight dip to the right, especially on special occasions. At this time of the year her monthly appointment was made with Christmas day in mind.

When Avis' hairdresser passed away twenty-six years ago, she was introduced to Cathy Greene, owner and stylist of Hair Focus. Avis was not only the most senior client, but she held the record for being the longest patron of the hair salon. Cathy liked to style Avis' hair with her back towards the mirror, then spin her around for the reveal.

"You should see the look on her face, she lights up the room with her smile."

Christmas morning always found Avis in church. She enjoyed Midnight Mass especially at St Mary's where parishioners gathered at 10 p.m. for carol singing. This was followed by the formal liturgy, the singing of hymns, the sermon, the prayers and the celebration of the Eucharist. The next few hours were spent resting, the mind trying to sleep while the rush of adrenalin kept the body awake in anticipation of the festive day ahead.

Before long, it is day break and already the hostess is preparing for the arrival of the family. She checks on every aspect of the setting, from the best crockery, cutlery and glassware to the themed placemats and napkins. A last-minute shift of some red poinsettia warms a dull corner. Family members arrive, each one with a specialty dish that completes the Christmas menu: baked turkey, ham, flying fish, green peas and rice, sweet potato, and jug-jug, a dish made from pigeon peas and guinea corn and flavoured with various meats and herbs. Avis' great cake is served for dessert; months before baking, the preserved fruit for this staple is soaked in port wine and rum. Her homemade sorrel, made with the sepals of the red flower and added spices, and spiked with a not-so-secret ingredient, was a favourite at Christmas.

The buffet of mouth-watering dishes is laid out. Avis makes one last touch, and then another, before she slips away. The family waits, huddled around the table. The delay of gustatory pleasure slows the clock and tests the patience, but for now this sight for hungry eyes and the aroma would have to suffice; until the air stirs, and like a butterfly fresh from its cocoon she emerges, a thing of beauty floating gently down the short hall way, as if on a breeze. A demure, yet charming smile acknowledges the wave of compliments; and then with bowed head, the matriarch and revered head of the household gives thanks for family and friends; she wishes them joy, peace and happiness in the coming year, and asks God's blessings on the meal.

The atmosphere is a mix of lively debate about both local and international issues, light-hearted banter and story-telling; tales of Ian's travel adventures; his arrest for jaywalking in Swaziland and being escorted to jail in a paddy wagon; or his trek into the Virunga National Park in Rwanda to spend time with the mountain gorillas. And occasionally, the group is treated to a collection of Ronnie's spectacular photos and video presentations that capture the spectacle of Christmas morning in Queen's Park.

Avis entertains with stories like the one about the workman who skilfully hopped on to the freshly-laid cream coloured carpet to avoid stepping on the shiny new strips of plastic that were there to protect it. But the grands find tales of their parents the most entertaining; like the tale of Ronnie the excavator. He was a creative child who had an eye for detail and a vision for landscaping spaces. Ronnie was determined to de-bush the area of overgrown foliage on the hill and level the yard directly behind the house. After much digging and shovelling, his younger brother by seven years grew concerned and warned the family that the excavation should cease; but he was only five years old and no one took his advice seriously, until a downpour of rain filled the depression, and inspired this ditty which Ian used to tease his brother every time they had a skirmish:

> If it is swimming yuh want to take
> Come leh we jump in Ronnie's lake.

The job that Ronnie started was eventually completed by experts and is now the main lawn to the east, sandwiched between the house and the school building.

This one we have heard several times, but it gets a chuckle every time it is told. At age five, Ian was a curious and talkative child who asked lots of questions. His Mum often mustered all the patience she could to indulge him, but on this occasion, he was chatting, the dog was barking, and she longed for some peace and quiet.

"Keep less noise, please," she pleaded.

"She says to keep less noise," he muttered to himself. "Does she mean me or the dog?"

"I mean whomever you think I mean," his mother replied sternly.

"Well then she must mean the dog."

And with that Ian continued his incessant chatter, bringing a warm smile to his mother's face. After many decades it still lingered just beneath the surface; it gushed into laughter and lit up her face every time she told the tale.

At times the roles were reversed, and the joke was on Mum. She often teased that none of the boys was handsome like their Dad.

"Because we look like our mother, that's why," Ian countered.

"Look, look, don't let me have to deal with you."

Her voice trailed as she tried to hold back a smile that threatened her attempt at being serious; then she shook her head in acknowledgement that Ian inherited his wit and story-telling charm from his mother.

In the midst of the jovial banter, an assortment of colourful bags and gift-wrapped boxes appears, as if on cue. The largest bags and the biggest boxes are reserved for the grandchildren. A suggestion to pool the money spent on gifts and give to charity was well received, but breaking with tradition took its time.

A new term starts in two weeks, and in five months the school would close its doors. For now, though, the reality of the future of Merrivale is drowned in the spirit of Christmas. It's Avis' happiest time of the year.

TWELVE

"It always seems impossible until it's done." —Nelson Mandela

Avis Carrington, the oldest graduate (Cohort 2, 1950), passes a symbolic torch to Reneaka Whittaker, the youngest graduate, class of 2018, Erdiston Teachers' Training College.

The End of An Era

THE students returned from the Christmas holiday break in early January 2010, as Avis and the home-school-family faced a major challenge. A stronger economy and higher incomes had afforded some parents greater choice among the private schools. Other parents, who had struggled to pay fees, opted for the government-sponsored public schools. These had improved significantly through extensive teacher-training programmes, and some were now among the top schools as measured by scores in the common entrance exam.

As the numbers declined, Avis was advised to close the school, or at the very least, reduce the number of staff members. Although this strategy had been tried before, and with success, she was adamant; the loyal teachers that had been with her, each for over thirty years, would be there to the very end.

Just after the Easter break, five students in Class 5 took the common entrance exam for transfer to the secondary level. The end-of-term party would soon follow; but this was not just the end of term, this was the end of an era, the last day of the iconic Merrivale Preparatory School. Parents were tense; they had been disappointed at the decision to close the school, and one family even made a generous donation to prolong what was inevitable.

The day was the 23 June, 2010, the last school day of school. Long, quiet faces and eyes on the brink of tears made clear the sombre mood for teachers and students. After all the years spent at Merrivale, "No one wanted to leave; it just did not feel right."

Miss Jones would make the last day a special one for Teacher; she sent invitations, a little late, but a small group of past students responded to the call. They assembled in the parking lot next door before making a surprise entrance. The party crashers arrived in an orderly line with the classic rush bottom chairs held over their heads, reminiscent of their walk to the end-of-term show many years ago. Teacher stood with eyes wide open and shook her head in disbelief as she was greeted with hugs, kisses and well wishes. They savoured every last moment, before nostalgia crept in.

"She was firm but sweet."

"You could not mess with her."

"She would move heaven and earth to get you to learn."

"She never gave up on you."

Speech-makers approached the podium spontaneously and praised Teacher for the school's many accomplishments. Miss Jones spoke on behalf of the teachers, and Mark Skinner, who wanted to quit school on the first day, spoke on behalf of the students. They thanked her for her dedication and how she had impacted their lives.

Teacher watched the show of talent and listened to the speeches. She was at times pensive but managed an occasional smile. She, in a slow walk across the room, met the children as they rushed to her side and clung as if never wanting to let go. Between hugs, she managed an emotional, "Thank you...all of you," and finally gave herself permission, to let a tear go.

The sadness was eventually interrupted with a long-held school tradition; the compilation of the hot dog list, which brought status to the person charged with the responsibility.

"How many of you are having hot dogs today?" And in that moment Lisa Clarke became the last person to compile the list at Merrivale.

Several hands shot up, before the order was rushed to Applewhaite, who was waiting to make the hot dogs as she had done for the last forty-four years. She too was saddened by the decision to close the school. She was very fond of the family and of Mrs Carrington in particular.

"I admired her a lot," she shared. "Especially her independence, her strength. Don't know where she got the energy." And after a slight pause and a chuckle, she added, "And of course, her style."

The excitement of planning for the graduation in two weeks delayed what was certain. The first ceremony was held in 1987 at the Dover Convention Centre. The girls wore lily white dresses accented with royal-blue corsages and the boys matched them in their crisply ironed white shirts, black pants and black bowties. Later traditional gowns would become the norm.

Graduation was different at Merrivale; there were students who were supported by a "big brother or big sister" and had either helped or had been helped by a peer. At this ceremony no child was elevated above the other, and no mention was made of individual performance, or the school to which each child was allocated. A journalist from one of the leading newspapers sought to highlight the top scorers in the common entrance exam; Mrs Carrington politely declined. This practice could have been a story of interest for educators and parents, but none was published.

On the 19th June, 2010, the last graduation ceremony was held at Merryhill, the headquarters of the Barbados Union of Teachers in Welches. None of the usual formality or ritual was spared for the small, final class of five: Shekinah Boyce, Chenille Callender, Kabira Foster,

Allyssa Reid, and Destiny Rogers. The girls were smartly turned out in their royal-blue academic gowns and tasselled mortar boards perched on their heads at just the right angle. They strutted confidently to the podium to receive a graduation scroll, and a gift of books, the same award given to each graduate of Merrivale.

Magistrate Barbara Cooke-Alleyne, QC (now the Registrar of the Supreme Court) gave the feature address. Angela Boyce, Shekinah's mother rendered Gloria Estefan's "Reach" which inspired the graduating class to "reach higher and be stronger." Kabira Foster's goodbye on behalf of the graduating class was a moving tribute in dance.

THIRTEEN

"She is clothed in strength and dignity, and she laughs without fear of the future." —Proverbs 31: 25

The Savannah Hotel, 2012. Starting in September of 2010, students arrange a luncheon and birthday outing for Teacher, seen here at centre wearing a pink top.

A New Dawn

THE bell that signalled the start of the school day is silent now. On 23 June, 2010, the curtain came down on an illustrious career that spanned a period of seventy-four years: twenty-three in the public service and fifty-one years of Merrivale Preparatory School. Family members were proud of her accomplishment, but felt a welcome sense of relief. At age ninety-one, just three months shy of her ninety-second birthday, Avis had passed the mandatory age of retirement in the government service by over twenty-five years. She was in good health, fully fit, with no major aches or pains, and was as passionate and committed to teaching as that first day in 1936 when she started her career at St Giles' Boys', and in 1959 when she welcomed the first students into her home. Her loyal staff of Mrs Holder, Miss Jones, Miss Williams, and Mrs Rock were still by her side. Teaching was her calling, her identity, her dream job. It was her life's work; but it was time.

"Shenstone" is quiet now—one of a few remaining family homes amidst the bustling business complex. Belleville became a "cultural heritage conservation area," according to the Amended Physical Development Plan 2003 of the Town and Country Development Planning

Office. Few of the iconic palms remain; they either succumbed to disease or were removed to make way for development. "Miss Walcott shop" at the corner of Pine Road is now closed, and part of the building is rented as apartments.

What survived the changes is the residential community at the southern corner of Pine Road. Medical and other commercial facilities now occupy renovated family homes or are housed in new architectural structures that must be built to specifications.

Gone from the family home is the collective hum of children at work, the sound of scurrying feet, and the chit-chat and laughter of children at play. The birds sing louder now, or so it seems; their calls once faded into the background noise. With the children gone, they flit freely in and out of the house, foraging for anything that is edible and even hop right up to a plate in the middle of a meal. On a morning that Avis was trying to steal a few more minutes of sleep, an audacious sparrow fluttered down from its perch and alighted on the bed. This wake-up call would have been welcomed on a workday.

"It's time to get up," it implied with its piercing tweet.

"Is it ever fair to call a bird a pest?" she asked herself as she made her way outdoors to welcome a new dawn.

Avis paused for a moment of reflection while tending the garden, this was her place of solace. How would she adjust to retirement after seven decades of teaching? Would she feel a sense of relief and embrace a life of leisure, or would there be feelings of loss? Most of these thoughts she kept to herself, well-guarded, but in other moments of introspection she wondered out loud:

"What am I going to do with all this free time?"

Erdine and Dan had grown into excellent cooks, but Avis always steered clear of the kitchen and readily admitted that her skills did not extend to anything culinary. While she enjoyed the Saturday run to the market, grocery shopping and food preparation were not her favourite chores. With the closure of the school and the departure of Applewhaite, who had prepared her meals for the last forty-four years, she was left with little choice. It was time for Avis to teach herself how to cook, and she would test her recipes on family members.

Avis quickly developed a few specialty dishes. A favourite was split pea soup served with sweet potato, yam and pigtails. She is still working on improving the dumplings; they continue to be a hit or miss. Another family favourite was a dish she simply calls potluck, made with spaghetti, vegetables, chicken, and bacon. It was served with a well-seasoned fried filet of Bangamary or flying fish, cucumber and pear (avocado) salad, and slices of sweet potato. The servings were encouraging, and Avis was motivated; yet, there remained all this "free time."

The advice from self-help books proved to be inadequate. Get a new job, they suggested, and for a short while Avis thought she could prolong an association with the old job by accepting an offer to tutor children twice a week. An appointment to arrange the sessions did not materialise, and the sense of relief she felt was seen as a sign to abandon the idea. She then thought to reverse roles and become the student; she would either acquire a second language, preferably Spanish, or improve her competence with the computer.

The technology advances of Avis' childhood were electricity and the telephone, and in her eighties, she was grappling with the invention of the modern era. The innovations fascinated her, there was the ease with which various tasks could be completed, and the unlimited availability of information at the end of a keystroke. Training at Erdiston was short term, and while she could manage the basics with the help of her daughter Shelley, she failed to achieve the mastery she desired.

On bad days, she fretted over those who excelled while she lagged behind, resigning herself to the notion that "competence is the preserve of the brilliant." On good days, Avis could be found on her laptop, typing a letter, researching a topic on Google, or watching a video clip of one of her icons, like Nelson Mandela, on YouTube. With a little assistance, she sometimes chatted with family members on Skype.

Whatever she chose, Avis knew it would not involve a new car. She gave up driving in 2009, due to what she called "divine intervention". When a driver reaches the age of seventy in Barbados, an eye test is mandatory before renewal of the licence. On the day of her test, she reached into her bag for her glasses. A search failed to find them hidden among the paraphernalia often found in the multiple compartments of a lady's handbag. At ninety-one years old, Avis took this as a sign that her driving days were over.

Fortunately, the bus stop across the street from her home provided access to the destinations she frequented; the minibus and the City Circle bus to Bridgetown; the Speightstown by-pass to the fish market at Oistins, Big B Supermarket (now Massy Stores) in Worthing in the south, and Holetown and Speightstown in the north of the island. And Avis took public transport to at least one funeral. She declined offers by family members and concerned past students who offered to provide taxi service, with all expenses paid. The independent retiree said this might curtail her activities and continued to use public transportation. Shelley retired in 2014, making it easier for her to get around.

This verse from "God's Garden" by Dorothy Frances Gurney, is one of Avis' favourites. It captures her love of horticulture:

> The kiss of the sun for pardon,
> The song of the birds for mirth,
> One is nearer God's heart in a garden
> Than anywhere else on earth.

After a breakfast of fresh fruit, and a cup of tea, Avis would hurry outdoors to greet the first light of the sun; the grass still wet with beads of overnight dew that reflect the dawn. Soon the busy street would be laden with pollutants from vehicles that line Pine Road from end to end; but for now, she could take a deep breath of the fresh air, to fuel the muscles, awaken the joints, and busy herself with garden work.

For a garden lover like Avis, the raking of leaves, the turning of soil, the repotting of plants, pruning a wayward branch, none of these was seen as a chore; and reference to her collection of books on gardening, *The Collingridge Encyclopedia of Gardening* or *House and Gardens A to Z of Plants* would easily help with the treatment of pests. Not so with the prolific giant African snail; with a voracious appetite for prized plants, or the bold green monkeys that raid the mango tree and slip into the house to steal bananas; these were more than a bother. Then there were two-legged pests who trespassed on the property, stealing plants, upending pots, taking garden tools and other implements. One arrived as a scammer, skilled at weaving a tale of misfortune in an attempt to secure a hand-out; but Avis would rather be "taken" than risk denying someone truly in need.

The Annual Flower Show at Ball's Plantation, Agrofest, Open Gardens and the Christmas season were annual events that refuelled her interest and passion in gardening.

The rewards were many; a struggling plant shows new life; a monarch butterfly flits by; an iridescent hummingbird shimmers in the sunlight; a floral shoot shows off its first flowers that add a splash of colour; a dot of green grows into a juicy mango; the essence of a bloom caught at the edge of a light breeze; the pleasure and the peace of time spent in the garden.

Retirement is a time to travel, but with trips to other Caribbean islands, across Europe, Canada and the United States, especially the annual trips to Miami for Christmas shopping, Avis had seen her share of the globe. Yet travelling remained on her list of favourite things to do, until the declaration that her travelling days were over. This was the first of many, that were voided once an opportunity was presented.

When Shelley attended business meetings in Washington in the summer of 2014, Avis went along for the ride.

Now in her in late nineties, Avis was erect in her posture and refused to use parking reserved for senior citizens, and objected to the use of a wheelchair when travelling abroad. It was after much persuasion that she eventually agreed, but the promised benefits fell woefully short of expectations. The assisted ride to the gate was uneventful, but as the time for departure drew near, inactivity at the booth alerted the travellers that they had been deposited at the wrong location. The wheelchair attendant had long gone, and the pair of Avis and Shelley ran the distance and were the last to board the flight from Miami to Washington. Avis was ninety-six years old; surely this would be her last trip, or so she professed. However, trips to Virginia in September of 2016 and to Michigan and Ontario in 2017 soon followed.

Travelling always provided Avis with the opportunity to indulge in her next favourite hobby, shopping. "I did not come up here to rest," she said once on a trip to Virginia. This was in response to a suggestion to shop only two out of a three-day cycle. "I can rest when I get back home." On her return to Barbados, an exhausted but satisfied nonagenarian spent a few days recovering from the ordeal.

A recent interest could hardly be called a hobby, because it did not appear to bring Avis any pleasure. Once her morning chores were done, she spent time positioned comfortably in front of the television to watch American politics. She sided with the Democrats and favoured Barack Obama in his bid to be the 44th President of the United States. Many persons in her age group never expected to see a black president in the White House in their lifetime.

Avis passionately discussed the current issues, complete with all of the key players.

"But, but tell me something, though", she would say, to get the conversation going. "How can John Boehner," then Speaker of the

House of Representatives, "say that Obama is hopelessly out of touch?" The Majority Whip, Mitch McConnell, former Vice-President Dick Cheney, Senator Ted Cruz, and others who opposed President Obama were drawn into her one-sided political rant. She could become so worked up that family members recommended that less time should be spent on CNN, Channel 201. This was unlikely to happen as Americans prepared for presidential elections in November 2016.

Avis watched every debate, knew every candidate on both sides of the aisle, and would have been delighted to witness the election of Hillary Rodham Clinton as the first female president of the United States.

"It's pure bad mindedness," she argued at the time. "You can tell me why Bernie Sanders is still in this race?" She held Senator Sanders responsible for the outcome of the election and preferred if his name was not mentioned in her presence. It took Avis a while to recover from the devastating loss of her candidate, but reasoned it was probably for her own good.

*

A promise to heed her family's advice saw a reduction in TV time; she rediscovered the joys of reading, and books and magazines again littered her bedside. The titled memoir, *What Happened*, authored by Hillary Clinton, had Avis glued to the television once again, as she anticipated the outcome of the investigation into Russian meddling in the 2016 election. The family eventually reserved their comments on her TV time. They reasoned that at her age, she had earned the right to watch what she wanted to watch, and for as long as she wanted.

The question of the "free time" may have been answered, but an additional concern soon became apparent. For the last seventy-four years, Avis Carrington looked forward to back-to-school, with its mix of anxiety and excitement. Anticipation of any likely obstacles were soon forgotten when the first child arrived, and the Merry in Merrivale returned. As the summer vacation of 2010 was coming to an end, the reality of her altered situation became evident. No longer would there be the smiles and the laughter of children at play, nor the greetings and the hugs that marked the start of a new school year. Avis became more aware that it was going to be unusually quiet at Number 15, Pine Road, causing a change in her refrain from,

"What will I do with all this free time?" to "What am I going to do come September?"

*

Lisa Clarke was a precocious four-year-old. When Teacher met her for the first time, she climbed into her lap, looked her fully in the eye and declared, "I love you, Teacher." She was not yet four-and-a-half, the requirement for whole-day school; but she won Teacher's heart and a place in the class of older children at Merrivale. The two developed a bond that has lasted ever since.

Lisa is the liaison between Teacher and alumni. She organised the group of past students who surprised Avis on the last day of school in June 2010, and was now the chair of an informal committee of four: Lisa, Steven Parris, Mark Skinner and Suzanne Workman, whose task was to solve the dilemma of September.

The committee knew that Teacher was very humble and did not like a lot of fuss.

They were careful to propose an activity that would meet with her approval. She eventually consented to a luncheon at Brown Sugar Restaurant three months after the school closed. The occasion has taken on the status of an annual luncheon held at a different venue each year: Accra Beach 2011, Savannah 2012, Mango Bay 2013, Sunbury 2014, Hilton Barbados Resort 2015, Divi South Winds 2016, and Crane Hotel 2017. This luncheon is held in September and also serves as a celebration of Teacher's birthday.

At times the monotony of Avis' retired lifestyle was pleasantly interrupted when former students or their parents stopped by the home. Some of these were chance occurrences; a past student would hop out of a fun walk or parade as it snaked its way along Pine Road, just to say a quick hello. Or a surprise visit like this one that caught Avis at home alone one quiet afternoon. There had been a breach of security a few weeks prior and when the doorbell rang, she cautiously opened the door a crack while securing herself behind the bolted wrought iron bars.

"We used to have two children at this school," she heard from a male voice with a British accent.

Using that old argument, that her housedress was not presentable, Avis peeked out from behind the door, making sure that only her face was visible. She rushed the conversation, but invited the Davies to join the family in celebrating Aunt Dan's birthday later that week.

Avis encountered members of the Merrivale family everywhere; at the supermarket, in the city, at social events, at funerals; and was often showered with hugs and kisses and tons of compliments. Former students marvelled at her youthfulness and style, her sharp memory and wit; how she could call them by name, and recall a funny tale or two out of school. A young boy rushed over to Avis at Agrofest, Barbados' main agricultural exhibition held in Queen's Park every February; the year was 2014.

"Do you remember me, Teacher?" he asked.

"Yes, of course, I remember you, JD."

His face lit up. He was seven years old when the school closed in 2010.

The phone call that started a warm and enduring friendship in the fifth year of Avis' retirement was not a chance encounter. Uncertain of the reception, Mary waited seventy years before building up enough courage to make the call.

"This is Mary Maycock Best. May I speak to Avis Carrington?" The connection was instant.

"My Mary?" she asked warmly. "Is this my goddaughter?"

At twenty-three years old, Avis had already earned a certain status as a respected teacher in her district. Young as she was, she did not quite understand the responsibility, but accepted politely, when Mrs Maycock asked her to stand as godmother for her daughter. When the child was still a toddler the family moved to Dash Valley in St George, and they lost contact.

All doubts and insecurities were erased when Mary met the family for the first time at a social gathering held at Ronnie's home, and Avis asked that her goddaughter sit right next to her. With daily calls to the Carrington home, the two soon became inseparable. "I thought I had lost you again," Avis expressed, on a day that she missed a call from Mary.

At age seventy-six, Mary's relatives were amazed that she had an active godparent with a social life. The two shared a love of gardening and could be seen at flower shows and open-garden events. Avis and her goddaughter enjoyed the seasonal recitals performed by The Wesley Singers and the Barclays Singers, and Mary became part of the family worship at the annual Anglican Diocesan Service held in February. When friends noticed that she had elevated her attire a notch, Mary explained, "My godmother is a dresser, and I have to keep up."

Iverton Newton described this visit as "one of the great encounters" of his life. He had not seen his "primary school teacher" since he left St Giles' Boys' in 1957, and she was certainly not in his thoughts when Mary took him to meet her ninety-nine-year old godmother. Sixty years had not dimmed his memory of Miss Inniss; an "amazing" and "truly great human being," a woman from whom he had learned grace, humility and charm. She was the only surviving teacher from his elementary school days, and he was able to thank her for the "gargantuan contribution" she made to his life and the lives of his classmates.

His thoughts were echoed by Dr Victor Eastmond. "She was the most beautiful teacher I had ever seen. She was firm, but gentle in her teaching manner." "We all wanted to listen to her and do well, get good marks". They both went on to the Lodge School and have remained friends. They both agreed that Avis Carrington had a profound effect on their lives.

*

Avis had avoided the limelight for several years, but she was gradually gaining celebrity status as her milestone hundredth birthday approached. She was featured in the 2017/2018 edition of *Fifty Plus* BARP (Barbados Association of Retired Persons) magazine; the article was reproduced in the 27 August, 2017, edition of The Nation Publishing Company's *Sunday Sun*. That November, she discussed her life as an educator in a Government Information Service broadcast titled, We Bajans. She made front-page news in *The Barbados Advocate* of 24 January, 2018, when she attended the 70th Anniversary service of Erdiston Teachers' Training College. Later that week Avis Carrington, the oldest remaining graduate of the college, passed the torch to the youngest graduate at the graduation ceremony for the Class of 2018.

At age ninety-nine, Avis was interviewed by Thomas King, a former student of Merrivale and a former head boy of Foundation School, for the Commonage project hosted by the Barbadian branch of the Royal Commonwealth Society. Older people from the Commonwealth, an organisation of Britain and former colonies of the British Empire, shared their life stories with young people. The essay titled "The Secrets to Longevity" was one of five from Barbados which appeared in *A Common Wealth of Experience*, published in 2019. Copies were presented to Queen Elizabeth II, all Commonwealth heads of government and those who were featured.

While anticipating her one-hundredth birthday, the family got a scare. As a young woman and especially during her three pregnancies, Dr Arnott Cato, later Sir Arnott was the family's physician. Avis enjoyed good health and had not seen a doctor in years, until a bout of bronchitis took her to Dr Carol Jacobs. The doctor was always satisfied with her general health and sometimes prescribed over-the-counter supplements, and Dr Beverly Barnett (Bev), Ronnie's wife, was sometimes consulted. This meant that a reluctant Avis paid few visits to her doctor of over twenty years, and only when symptoms persisted.

Avis was sure that she had caught a bone in her throat, but decided not to alarm the group that had met for lunch. The following morning the irritation was still present, and a visit to FMH Emergency Medical Clinic confirmed her fears. The bone was stuck in the soft tissue and had to be removed surgically, and under general anaesthesia. A few weeks earlier she had choked on a capsule. Luckily, Ronnie was present and applied the Heimlich Manoeuvre to dislodge the object. Shelley immediately completed training in First Aid and the countdown to her milestone continued.

FOURTEEN

"He who is of calm and happy nature will hardly feel the pressure of age." —Plato

Avis with the Governor General Dame Sandra Mason on the occasion of her centenary, September 2018.

One Hundred Years

AVIS used the same tired argument, "I don't like the limelight," "I don't like any fuss." "And certainly," she admonished her children, "No visit from the Governor General." Her sister Constance Inniss (Dan), had made the same request three years ago and had her wish granted. She was featured when the Barbados Postal Service issued a limited stamp edition, "Centenarians of Barbados," to pay tribute to citizens who had reached that milestone. The children refused to take "no" for an answer and with gentle and gradual coaxing, Mum softened her position and celebrated one hundred years with pomp and ceremony. "My children are very good to me and have always been supportive," she reasoned. "I started to think it would be ungracious of me not to grant them their wish to celebrate this milestone."

Eventually Avis became very involved in the preparations, wanting to know every detail, making her own suggestions, and trying to scale back some of the planned events that would be held in her honour. And soon she was looking forward to the visit from the Governor General, and wondering out loud if the Honourable Dame would accept an invitation to see her garden.

Avis was the centre of attention in a cream-coloured pair of slacks, a cotton-knit blouse that showed a hint of shoulder, and a long sleeveless duster jacket with bold black, green and red embroidery on either side of the front panels. It was the eve of her hundredth birthday and the congregants, a mix of church members, family, friends, former teachers, former students and their parents, met at St Cyprian Church, where she had been a member for fifty-nine years, for a service that started the celebrations.

Avis Carrington "was worthy of emulation," said the officiating priest Reverend Joseph King in his sermon, "The Taming of the Tongue." "In her ministry of teaching," he continued, "she used her tongue in uplifting and positive ways; to impart knowledge, to encourage, to comfort and to discipline when necessary." He then instructed the worshippers, "Encourage others with our words or say nothing at all."

At the end of the service the Acting Governor General, Sir Kenneth Hewitt, a former student of St Giles' Boys' and a Merrivale parent, broke with protocol and warmly embraced the birthday girl. Later that Sunday evening, Avis was toasted at a cocktail reception held in her honour and serenaded by two renowned musicians and former Merrivale students, Nicholas Branker and Arturo Tappin.

One of the fun moments came when the master of ceremonies for the night, her son Ian, probably in a bid to get back at his mother, revealed what was up until that time, a well-guarded secret: his mother's given name. Ian regretted that his grandfather passed away before he was born; but with names like Avisene Caeseretta, who preferred to be called Avis, and Constance Lesoline Leola who was called Dan, it was probably fortunate that Robert Inniss was not around to have a say in the choice of his name. But Avis would have the last word. She told the often-repeated story about the day that Ian was chatting and the dog was barking; and soon ripples of laughter filled the room.

The preparations for the Governor General's visit started weeks in advance with security checks, the provision of special furniture, recommendations for the type of non-alcoholic wine for toasting and protocols to be observed. On 17 September, 2018, Avis Carrington celebrated her birthday with the Honourable Dame Sandra Mason, parliamentary representative for the constituency, the Honourable Marsha Caddle, friends and relatives, some travelling from abroad for the occasion: From the United States, her son Ian and wife Hazel, adopted son Melvin, and Mrudula, who also lived with the Carringtons, and her husband Praveen; from Toronto, Canada her grandson Julian and his mother Phillipa; Lawrence, Vere's nephew, and his wife Cecile travelled from Trinidad and Tobago.

For the occasion, Avis chose a thin strap bohemian sun dress in bold patterns of pink burgundy and gold, accentuated with a rust-coloured scarf draped over the right shoulder. A strappy wedge heeled shoe and a bold three-tiered bronze necklace completed the look. "She did dress real young, dressed like she ready to hit the town, not like the 'hundredarians' who does dress up in church clothes. Like if they going to a funeral," Eric Lewis commented in his weekly column in *The Nation*. Her strong voice, youthful spirit, sharp wit and memory caused many to aspire to be like her, even as they questioned her age. "I want to look just like she when I reach a hundred." "I would have to see she birth certificate."

As if providing proof of Avis' age, the Governor General opened her remarks by assuring those gathered that she had indeed seen the evidence. After the formalities, a letter from the Queen of England was read, a bottle of wine and a bouquet of flowers were presented, followed by the speeches and the toast. Her Excellency accepted a prearranged invitation to stroll through the garden that had been primped for the occasion. The celebrations continued later that day with a family luncheon at Champers restaurant.

Avis was a picture of casual elegance in a candy-striped skirt cinched at the waist with a black sash and an off-the-shoulder white cotton blouse with layered ruffled sleeves. Avis was touched when the

Honourable Prime Minister of Barbados Mia Mottley joined the party on her way home from a business trip. In her remarks she lauded Teacher, not only for her vitality and fashion, but for the essence of who she was.

"I did all that I could to get here because, other than my parents and my grandmother, I don't know that I could place the responsibility for being who I am, more than with Mrs Carrington. And the older I become, the more I realise how true that is." She admired Teacher for developing human beings and allowing children to be the best that they could be; for the nurturing, the patience, the understanding, and noted that, "Those who dared to be different were never suppressed."

In her response, Avis treated the guests to a tale out of school. Mia was one of several children who were all tell-tale-tits, doing their little part to be the extra eyes and ears to ensure that there was good behaviour at all times, but also keeping Teacher busy with their minor complaints. "Teacher, somebody pinch me." "Somebody took my pencil." "I saw someone going up the hill."

"You don't have to tell me, you can speak to them," she said to Mia after a complaint was reported.

"But I speak to them and they don't listen to me," Mia replied.

"Well now," Mrs Carrington said, beaming with admiration, "all of Barbados is listening to Mia Mottley."

The closure of the school in 2010 left Avis with a feeling of emptiness at the beginning of the new school year; this had been resolved with an annual luncheon each September. The ninth annual luncheon was a celebration of Teacher's one hundredth birthday. The Aquatic Club Restaurant of the Radisson Aquatic Resort could not accommodate the number of past students who wanted to celebrate with the new centenarian.

In his tribute, Andrew Pilgrim noted that, "Mrs Carrington produced an exceptional group of young people, at a time when there was the view, right or wrong, that people of our hue were not exposed to excellent education in the way that we were." He thanked Mrs Carrington for a significant part of his confidence and the joy in his life, all the result of his days at Merrivale. "We love you; we thank you; we always will remember you."

But it was Angela Beckles' story that resulted in a wave of emotional "Aws," and a round of applause. Just before leaving for secondary school she was summoned to see Teacher. Children had a way of exaggerating the message, so she approached with apprehension, thinking maybe she was in trouble.

In the gentlest and most caring voice, Teacher explained that her house had burnt down. She was comforted and arrangements were made to take her home. "A week after," Angela continued, "you took me shopping at Cave Shepherd." Her memories of the visit to the department store on Broad Street in Bridgetown remain fresh.

"Can anyone remember me from school?" This question was posed by Frank Callender, a former student of St Giles' Boys' who heard of the event and dropped by to offer congratulations. "There was life before Merrivale," he continued. "I remember a twenty-six-year year old Ms Inniss, a beautiful lady who the youngsters adored and who left a lasting impression."

Some of the warmth and celebration was reserved for "Applewhaite." The specially invited guest of honour was seated right next to Mrs Carrington. This was quite a surprise for the Merrivale alumni. She had been a constant in their primary school life, and they were delighted to see her after so many years.

Ice blocks wrapped in foil, reminiscent of school days, were specially ordered as part of the dessert. And everyone joined in the singing as "Puff the magic dragon" was revisited as he "frolicked by the sea," and "Zip a dee doo dah," was a fitting ending to a "wonderful feeling and a wonderful day."

Avis' hundredth birthday gained her media attention; and after spending her life avoiding the limelight, she had become the nation's sweetheart. She was stopped, pointed at, gawked at, showered with compliments, and occasionally greeted with the birthday song. Her initial reaction was to avoid the attention, but she quickly learned to embrace it. At an open garden event, admirers, cell phones at the ready, asked her to be part of their "selfies."

The stylish centenarian was also highlighted in a photo shoot titled "Bajan Girls Rock, Independence Edition" by prominent fashion designer Pauline Bellamy, in honour of her hundredth birthday and the conferment of the Dame of St Andrew. The gown was inspired by traditional Barbadian architecture and captioned "Growing bolder, not older. Dame Avisene Carrington proves that beauty can be eternal." This along with images of Avis being feted and celebrated were posted on Facebook, Instagram, WhatsApp and other social media sites, and seen across the globe.

At one hundred years of age, Avis was often asked about the secret to her youthfulness and always insisted there was none; but her genetics and her lifestyle may have contributed to her longevity. Her cousin Louis, who spent weekdays at the Inniss home, and her sister Dan were centenarians. And Avis always had an active life. She retired from teaching three months shy of her ninety-second birthday; she spent more time gardening, continued her weekly runs to Cheapside and the supermarket, and made the occasional shopping trip to Bridgetown.

Avis must have benefitted from a healthy diet. This was not prescribed; anything that got her in and out of the kitchen quickly was preferred; small portions of basic foods like rice, potatoes, pasta, fish, and chicken, and she loved fruits and vegetables. In contrast, she readily admitted to a having a sweet tooth; her tea and homemade drinks were always laden with sugar, and her candy box was always packed with chocolate-filled mint candy and stacks of Oh Henry bars made of chocolate, nuts and fudge; and she could whip up a marble cake, or an apple pie and add a scoop or two of vanilla ice cream.

Avis had only a few close friends. She met Hildegarde Weekes at St Michael's Girls' School, Iris Riley at St Giles' Boys' and Muriel Norgrove was her dorm mate at Erdiston; they all predeceased her. Left with no choice, she surrounded herself with "younger people."

"Age is not a factor," she stated when discussing the relationship with her daughter-in-law. "I don't understand why she wants to go out with me. We have a lot in common, so age is just a number."

Avis had a calm, sweet and gentle spirit, and always considered herself blessed, knowing that her faith had kept her over the years. And she never forgot to offer sincere thanks to those who helped her on this long, at times challenging and painful, yet exciting and adventurous, purposeful and fulfilling journey that was her life of one hundred years.

FIFTEEN

"The desire to reach for the stars is ambitious.
The desire to reach hearts is wise." —Maya Angelou

Former student of Merrivale, The Honourable Mia Mottley, Prime Minister of Barbados with Teacher on her 100th birthday, 17 September, 2018. The Prime Minister was on her way back from an overseas business trip.

Reflections

LOOKING back on her long life, Avis marvels at how the pieces fit together, as if ordained. She endured a miserable elementary school life, and at the secondary level she experienced a redemption that sparked an interest in teaching. She was mentored at the top elementary school by one of the education greats of the day, and trained at Erdiston, the premier teacher's training college in the region. And there remains a tinge of disbelief, that the small playgroup started to appease her three-year old son mushroomed into Merrivale Preparatory School, which has left its mark on the education landscape of Barbados, and well beyond.

The island was a British colony when Avis was born in 1918, one week after the end of the First World War. In 1937, her walk to the Bridgetown library was halted on the first day of the Bridgetown riots that led to social and economic change. She was twenty-one when the Second World started and observed the "lights out" to keep enemy aircraft at bay; and was one week shy of her twenty-fourth birthday when the Canadian steam ship *Cornwallis* was torpedoed in Carlisle Bay by a German U-Boat, a submarine used in the war. In 1955 Avis was pregnant with her second son when she witnessed the devastation of hurricane Janet, which left thirty-eight dead, and over two thousand homeless. The rented family home at Two Mile Hill in St Michael suffered no damage, and provided refuge for two families for a couple of weeks.

Avis was thirty-four years old when universal adult suffrage allowed women to vote in political elections, a right previously extended to male landowners. She was present for the installation of Grantley Adams, the first premier of Barbados, and the failed attempt at a Federation of the West Indies under his leadership. She celebrated the birth of the nation in November 1966 with the nation's first Prime Minister, and Father of Independence, Errol Walton Barrow. When the Barbados Labour Party won the 2018 general election, Avis celebrated a century of change, from limited access to schooling and job opportunities for girls to the swearing-in of her former student Mia Amor Mottley as Barbados' first female Prime Minister.

Avis was delighted with the developments in education post-Independence. Government-sponsored education was guaranteed for all, regardless of race, social class, or gender. By September 2015, the last year for which statistics were available, approximately 50,000 students were enrolled at ten public pre-primary, sixty-eight public primary and twenty-one government secondary schools. Public tertiary-level education was offered at Barbados Community College, Samuel Jackman Prescod Institute of Technology, Erdiston Teachers' Training College and the regional University of the West Indies.

Salaries have increased over the years, with males and females eventually earning equal pay for equal work. Women have served at the highest levels of education administration, as Permanent Secretary, Chief Education Officer and Minister of Education. Avis was equally fascinated by the integration of technology into the teaching and learning process, especially the possibilities for the future.

Nevertheless, her heart still yearned for an alternative to the common entrance exam. Every year she agonised over the anxious students who were eager to please their parents, some carrying the guilt of not living up to expectations; and she was saddened by the way that some parents demonstrated their disappointment. "The exam is too much for the average child," she said. "On reflection, this is not good for children. Those who do not make it to the 'top schools' feel less worthy, as if they are second-class citizens. These children are set adrift. The system is failing them." And in a defiant tone, as if addressing the policy-makers, she stated emphatically, "The exam has served its time."

Every day that she rose, her heart was full of gratitude for her long life. Except for the occasional, unexplained allergic reaction and cramping in the legs, Avis was thankful for her good health. She took her aging in stride, fully embracing the reality of her mortality. "I don't know how long I have on this planet, so I am requesting that family members worship with me once a year, and join me for lunch afterwards. It means a lot to me." Not that there was anything morbid in the way she made the statement. It was just part of the premise, on which the invitation to the annual Anglican Diocesan service in February rested; and the start of the latest Carrington family tradition.

As she reflects on a century of memories, she debunks a long-held ritual. "There must be no eulogy at my funeral," she states, not pausing for opinions. "These were just the things I wanted to do, and there is no need for anyone to be talking about it." The room becomes uncomfortably quiet, until there is a change in subject and the conversation comes back to life.

*

Avis left a mark on the education landscape in Barbados through her service in public schooling and the founding of Merrivale Preparatory School. To her students she was a firm, strict, no-nonsense disciplinarian, yet she was loving, kind, patient, understanding and nurturing.

She was gracious and graceful, and worthy to be emulated. She was a phenomenal teacher; and the one who had the greatest positive impact on their journey through formal education. Most of all, they remembered the special interest Teacher showed; and that she never gave up on a single child. That was the essence of Avis Carrington and the magic of Merrivale.

"What is your legacy?" she was asked.

"What legacy what?" She objects with a humility that is almost dismissive.

"Dame Avisene?" A tease to remind her that she received the prestigious honour for her contribution to early childhood and primary education in Barbados.

"It was never about me," she says, continuing: "Observing how a young child grows and blossoms into a flourishing spirit; to watch them develop and pursue their dreams and make a contribution to the society; the joy of knowing that you contributed in some small way is immeasurable."

"How do you want to be remembered?"

The response comes without hesitation.

"Simply as 'Teacher.'"

And in a moment of prayerful reflection, she acknowledges she has answered the call and accomplished her purpose.

"This is what God required of me."

Teacher.

Fond and familiar faces.

Above left: Ms Ruby Applewhaite receives an award for 33 years of devoted service as housekeeper and cook, from The Honourable Mia Mottley, then Minister of Education, during the school's 40th anniversary celebrations.

Above right: Lisa Clarke visits her favourite teacher just days before Merrivale's final day of school.

Opposite top: Avis, second from right, on a day out with "young" friends. From left, goddaughter Mary Best, niece Hazel Byer-Horsford, daughter Shelley and family friend Carol Phillips.

Opposite: Annual luncheons began after the school closed in 2010 to answer Avis' question, "What am I going to do come September?"

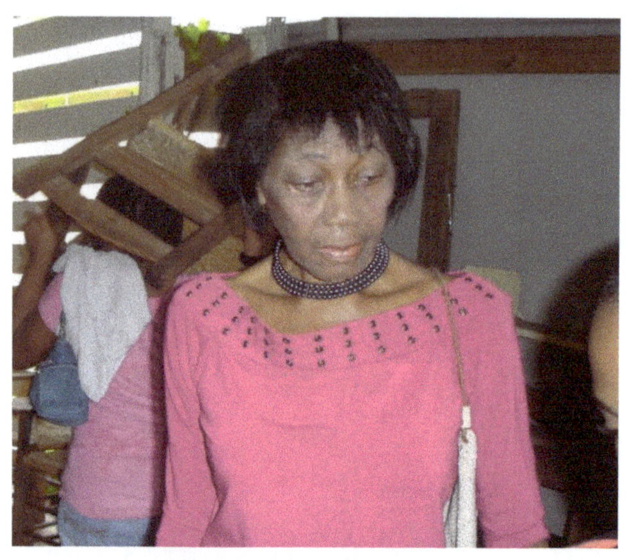

The last day.

Top: Teacher with tear-filled eyes, 23 June, 2010.
Above: Children say goodbye.

The last graduating class, July 2010.

From left: Chenille Callender, Allyssa Reid, Destiny Rogers, Kabira Foster and Shekinah Boyce.

Stunning and stylish at any age.

Above: Avis dressed for the opening ceremony of the Queen Elizabeth Hospital, 1964.

Above right: Escorted by her son Ronnie during the 40th anniversary celebrations.

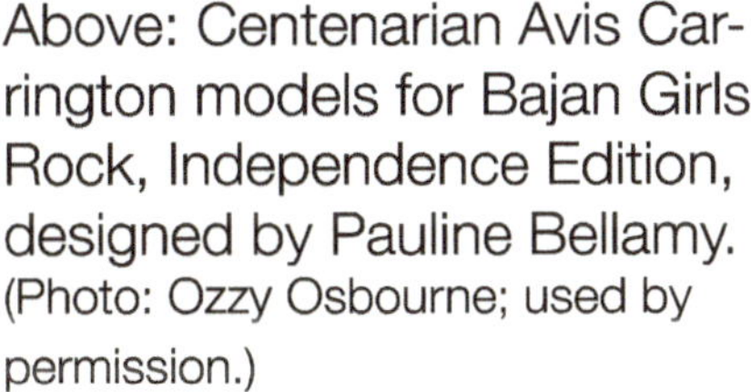

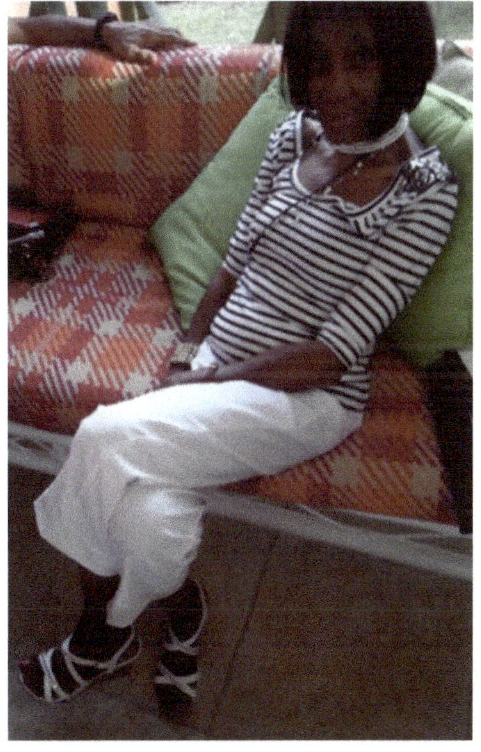

Above: Centenarian Avis Carrington models for Bajan Girls Rock, Independence Edition, designed by Pauline Bellamy. (Photo: Ozzy Osbourne; used by permission.)

Top right: Avis attended the wedding of former student Charmaine Fleming in Michigan, USA, June 2017.

Right: Ever the fashionista, Avis bought a plain pair of white sandals and added the bling!

References

Allsopp R. S. R. (ed.). (1996). *Dictionary of Caribbean Usage*. Oxford University Press. New York.

Bancroft, B. (2015, April 27). http://bancroft.berkeley.edu/ROHO/ wgmnpapers/marychamberlainpaper.pdf

Barbados Boy Scouts Association Scouts. (2015, March 3). http://bbsascoutcommittee.org/

Barbados. *Education Commission Report*. (1876). Xerox copy of reprint which appeared in the Bulletin: A periodical for teachers in Barbados 2, 2-3. 1954-55.

Carter, H. (2004). *Shaping a Nation. Principals of Barbados 1900 – 1980. Volume 1. Barbados*. The Barbados Government Information Service.

Central Bank of Barbados (2019, April 3).
http://www.centralbank.org.bb/news/article/9461/45-things you-
didn't-know about-Barbados-money.

Cole, J. (1982). Official ideology and the education of women in the
English-speaking Caribbean, 1835-1945, with special reference to Barbados. In *Women and Education*. Bridgetown, Barbados: University of
the West Indies, Cave Hill, Institute of Social and Economic Research.

Cutteridge, J. O. (1921, October 2). Elementary Teachers' Union.
Tribute to the late Mr. L. N. Carrington. Trinidad Guardian.

Fraser, H., & Hughes R. (2008). *Historic Houses of Barbados.*
Wordsmith International.

Global Initiative to End All Corporal Punishment at School (2015,
May 13).
http://www.endcorporalpunishment.org/pages/hrlaw/crcsession.html

Gordon, S. C. (1963). *A century of West Indian education.* London:
Longman Group Ltd.

Government of Barbados (1945). A policy for education. Bridgetown,
Barbados; Department of Education: Author.

(1978). The Report of the National Commission on the Status of
women in Barbados: Vol. 2. Bridgetown, Barbados: Ministry of the
Attorney General. Bridgetown, Barbados. Author.

(1995). The White Paper on Education Reform. Ministry of Education, Youth Affairs and Culture. Bridgetown, Barbados. Author.

(2004). *Historical Developments of Education in Barbados 1686-2000.* Ministry of Education, Youth Affairs and Sport. Bridgetown, Barbados. Author.

(2008). The development of education. National report of Barbados. Ministry of Education, Human Resource and Development. Bridgetown, Barbados. Author.

Inniss, J. W. (1992). *The Development of Erdiston Teachers' Training College 1948-1992.*

Larry, H., & Silbar, J. (1982). Wind Beneath My Wings. [Recorded by Midler, B.]. On *Beaches*, original soundtrack. [CD]. New York, N.Y. Rhino Atlantic. 1988

Leatham, R. E. (2015, May 13). http://www.hymnary.org/text/thankyoufortheworldsosweet.

Lewis, E. (2018, November 28). Bajans too like to eat. Weekend Nation, pp.11.

Merrivale Preparatory School (1999). Merrivale Preparatory School 40th Anniversary Commemorative Booklet.

Ministry of the Attorney General. (1992). Education Legislation of 1982. CAP 41. The laws of Barbados. Bridgetown, Barbados: Author.

Small, Y. A. *The Role of Private Primary Education in Barbados; A*

Case Study of Vale Preparatory School. Unpublished master's thesis. Concordia University, Montreal, Quebec, Canada.

The Girl Guides Association of Barbados (2015, March, 10). http://girlguidesbarbados.org/about-us.html

Town and Country Planning Development Office. (2015, April, 2). http://www.townplanning.gov.bb/downloads/BellevilleLocalareaPlan.pdf

Wickham, P. (2015, May, 13). https://www.nationnews.com/nationnews/news/57368/people-views-flogging

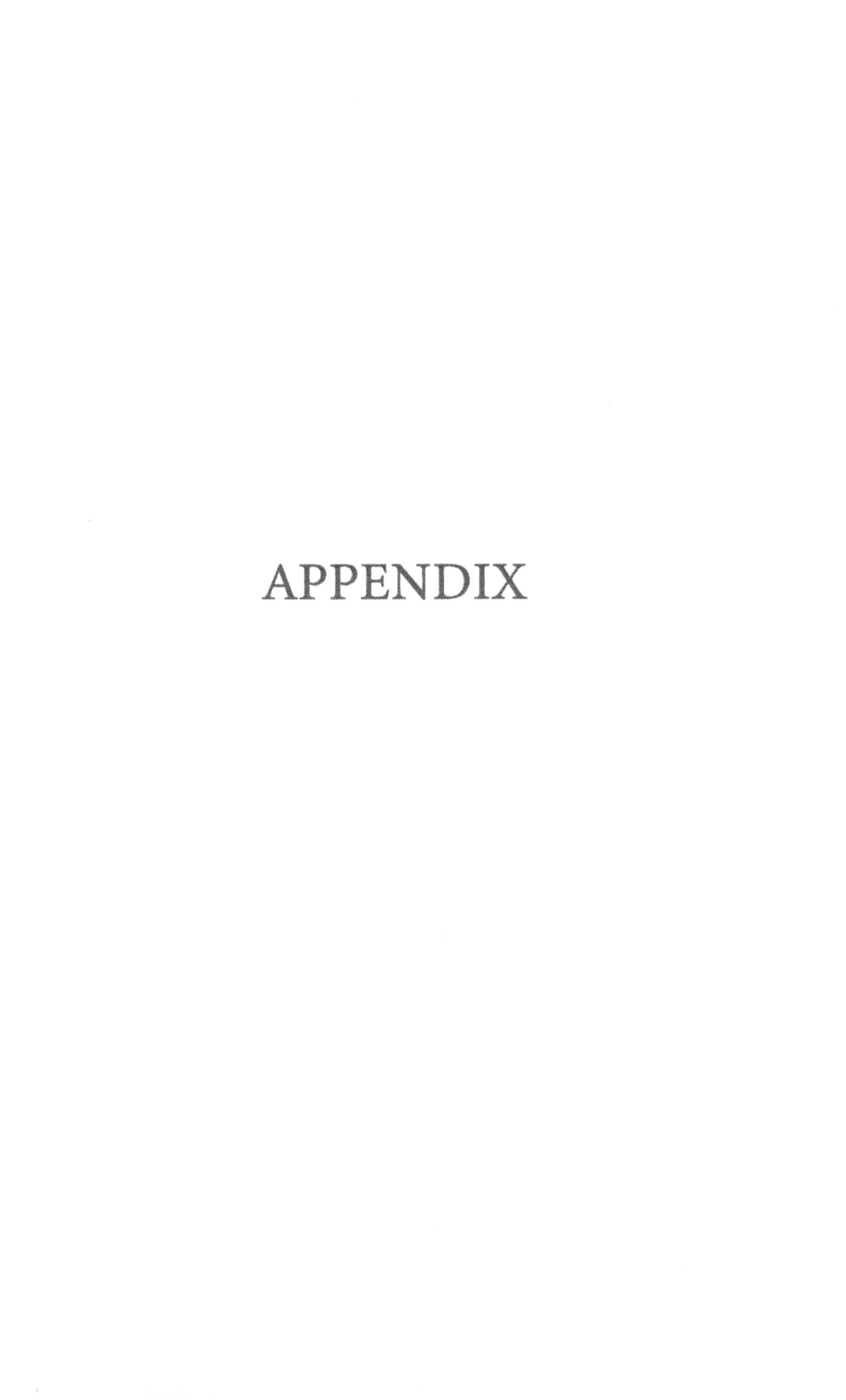

APPENDIX

Fig. 1

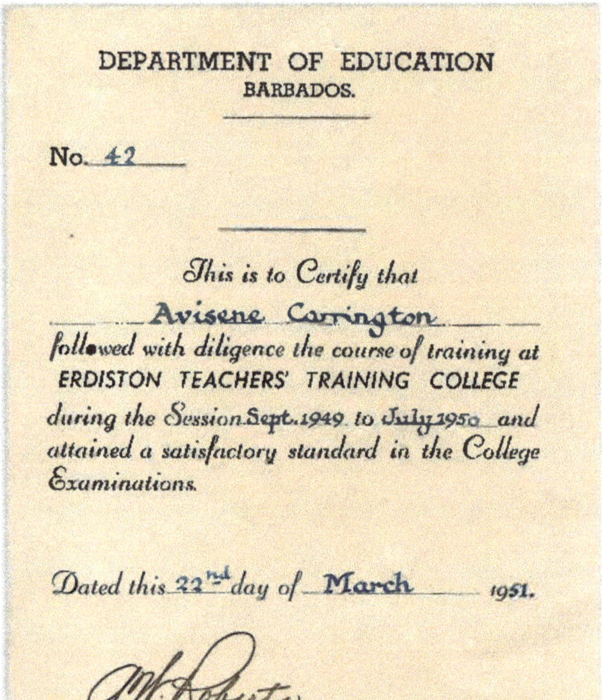

DEPARTMENT OF EDUCATION
BARBADOS.

No. 42

This is to Certify that

Avisene Carrington

followed with diligence the course of training at
ERDISTON TEACHERS' TRAINING COLLEGE
during the Session Sept. 1949 *to* July 1950 *and attained a satisfactory standard in the College Examinations.*

Dated this 22nd *day of* March 1951.

A.W. Roberts
Principal

Director of Education.

Avis Carrington was awarded the Teachers' Certificate from Erdiston Teachers' Training College in 1950.

Fig. 2

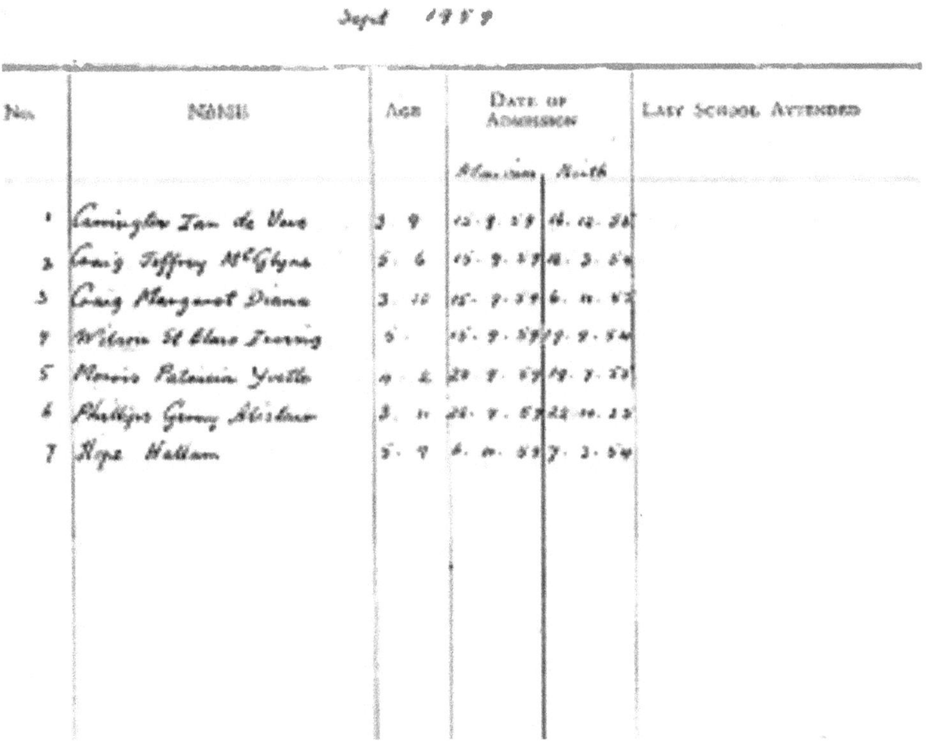

Sept 1959

No.	Name	Age	Date of Admission	Birth	Last School Attended
1	Carrington Ian de Vere	3 9	12. 9. 59	16. 12. 55	
2	Craig Jeffrey McGlynn	5 6	15. 9. 59	18. 3. 54	
3	Craig Margaret Diana	3 10	15. 9. 59	6. 11. 55	
4	Wilson St Clair Irving	5	15. 9. 59	19. 9. 54	
5	Morris Patricia Yvette	4 2	28. 9. 59	19. 7. 55	
6	Phillips Gerry Alistair	3 11	28. 9. 59	22. 10. 55	
7	Hope Hallam	5 9	6. 10. 59	7. 3. 54	

Enrolment, September 1959. The first seven students of Merrivale School

Figs. 3 & 4

Teaching resources at Merrivale School:

Nelson's West Indian Readers. First Primer. J O Cutteridge, Author. Pages 2 and 5 (Source: https://books.google.com/books?id=ivGkL7gO-ZJUC&printsec=frontcover&source=gbs_ge_summary_r&cad=0#v=onepage&q&f=false)

Pages from a Janet and John book. (Source: https://www.amazon.com/Janet-John-Off-Play-Books/dp/1840246154)

Fig. 5

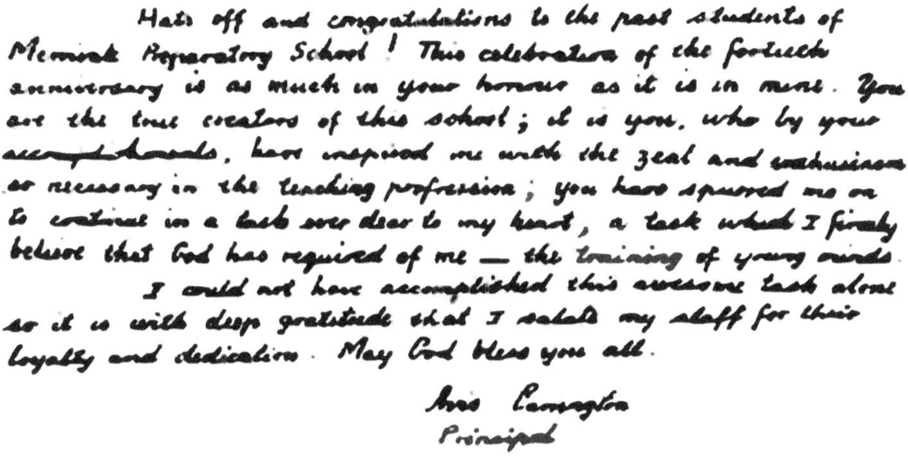

Hats off and congratulations to the past students of Merrivale Preparatory School! This celebration of the fortieth anniversary is as much in your honour as it is in mine. You are the true creators of this school; it is you, who by your accomplishments, have inspired me with the zeal and enthusiasm so necessary in the teaching profession; you have spurred me on to continue in a task ever dear to my heart, a task which I firmly believe that God has required of me — the training of young minds.

I could not have accomplished this awesome task alone so it is with deep gratitude that I salute my staff for their loyalty and dedication. May God bless you all.

Avis Carrington
Principal

Handwritten message from Avis Carrington on the 40th anniversary of the school.

Source: Merrivale Preparatory School 40th Anniversary commemorative booklet, 1999.

Fig. 6

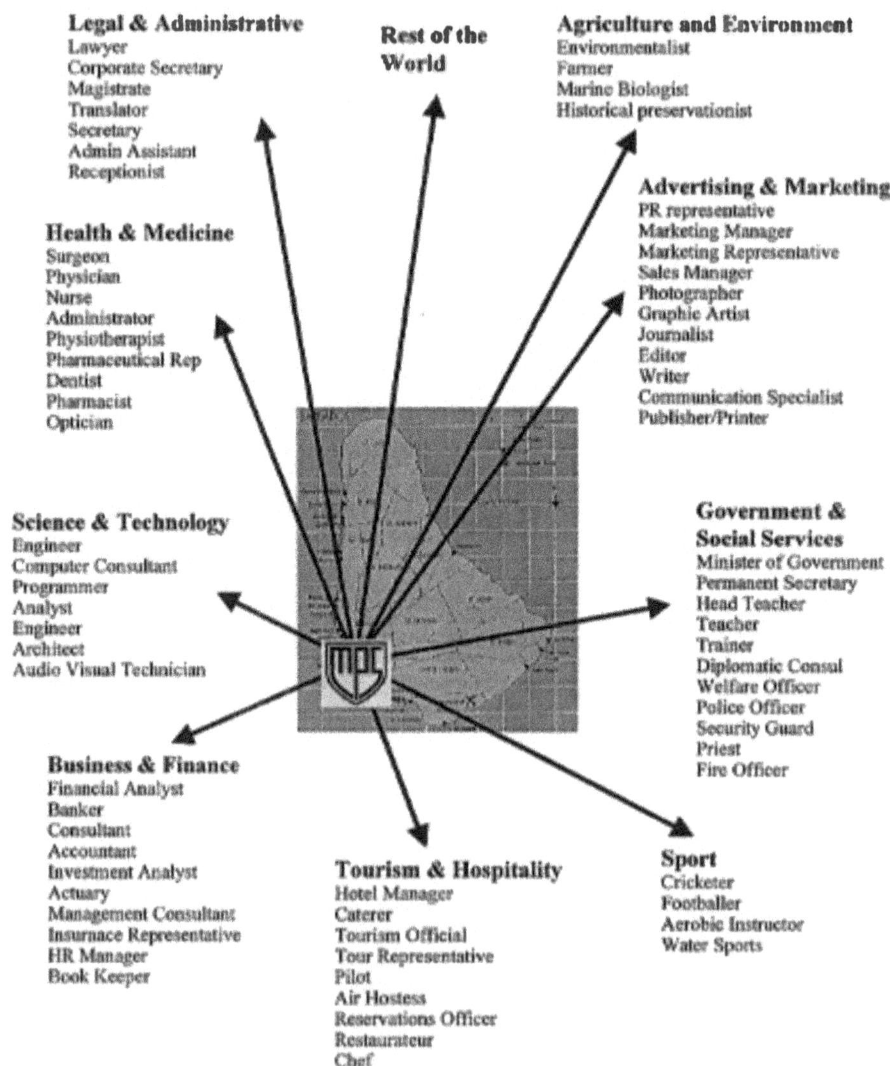

Source: Merrivale Preparatory School 40th anniversary
commemorative booklet, 1999.

Fig. 7

Programme for the last graduation ceremony, Merrivale Preparatory
School, 19 June, 2010.

ABOUT THE AUTHOR

HAZEL Lindo-Carrington is an educator who started her career as a teacher of science at Boys' Foundation School. Students found her approach "creative," "dynamic" and "refreshing," as she sought to develop their individual strengths and foster independent thought.

Her interest in students led her beyond the confines of science education to a broader concern with social issues that impact education. To this end, she completed a Doctor of Philosophy in Education from the University of the West Indies, Cave Hill Campus, specialising in sociology of education broadly, with an interest in gender and boys' academic achievement in particular.

Dr Lindo-Carrington has served as a resource person at the School of Education, UWI, Cave Hill, with brief stints as tutor at Erdiston Teachers' Training College, where she has trained and mentored student teachers. Her hobbies are gardening, reading, and writing dialect poetry.

But what really gets her adrenalin flowing is the dynamic of the classroom. For in her heart of hearts, at the very core, she is a proud teacher.